A Poet And A Killer

Jessi Dillard

Published by Pettway Publishing, 2021.

While every precaution has been taken in the preparation of this book, the publisher assumes no responsibility for errors or omissions, or for damages resulting from the use of the information contained herein.

A POET AND A KILLER

First edition. June 29, 2021.

ISBN: 979-8224630486

Written by Jessi Dillard.

A POET AND A KILLER

JESSI DILLARD

1

Known by many as the Poet Laureate of America's Damned, Stephen Wayne Anderson had a talent for expressing himself with words – earning himself plenty of awards and admiration despite the fact that his literary masterpieces were written while he awaited execution on death row.

In fact, Anderson's knack for language allowed him to innately capture the feelings of despair, hopelessness, and regret that were abundant among the condemned. His elegant prose even led many to believe that he must have been wrongly charged – anyone who could write such brilliant, sympathetic poetry certainly wouldn't have been able to commit the act of murder?

"I miss listening to the sounds of night, crickets chirping and birds calling each other, I miss watching life unfold and hearing echoes continuing through winter's cold," reads one of Anderson's verses. "I miss so much living behind these walls, cloistered away from the world beyond: but sometimes I hear the rain across the roof, and smell it upon the sidewalks cleaned."

There was no way, they argued, that this poet with an IQ of 136 could possibly be the same person who had been in and out of prison for more than half his life – and who was responsible for the cold-blooded killing of an innocent grandmother.

A fugitive at 26

In 1953, in St. Louis, Stephen Wayne Anderson was the first of two sons born to a couple who struggled with significant mental instability. His father was an angry alcoholic who struggled to control his temper – and usually failed. His mother detested her children so much that she would regularly tell them that she "dreaded the days" she'd given birth to them.

The beatings and abuse were frequent, but Anderson did his best to shield his younger brother from the worst of it – until, at age 14, he was kicked out of the family home. At that time, they were living in New Mexico.

Anderson fled into the hills, where he learned to rely on his wits and good fortune. He also learned how to steal, and was convicted of burglary and thrown in a Utah jail by the time he was 18 years old. He wasn't there long, however – by November 1979, he broke out after assaulting a corrections officer and one inmate, and murdering another.

"When I escaped, walked away, however you want to look at it, from the Utah State Prison, they were looking for me – the law enforcement authorities were looking for me," he said in a statement to police after his final arrest. "And these people hid me. And they went through a lot. They – in fact, one man's house, I guess you can call it – raided, because they thought I was there.

"And I stayed in the mountains in Mill Creek Canyon for several days. And they supplied me with what I needed and took care of me. And then, eventually got me out of town, when the heat died down."

He managed to fly under the radar for a few months. However, on Memorial Day weekend in 1980, a call came in to the police from the concerned neighbours of an 81 year old retired piano teacher named Elizabeth Lyman. According to the report, the neighbours had peeked out the window after hearing dogs barking, and saw a suspicious looking man inside the elderly woman's house.

Officers showed up soon after, where they discovered Anderson – already a fugitive at the age of 26 – sitting in the kitchen of Lyman's Bloomington, California, home. He was casually eating a bowl of noodles and drinking a glass of milk while watching television.

He told the authorities that he'd broken into the house to steal Lyman's money – he'd thought that Lyman was away on holiday. However, the officers noted that prior to entering the home, Anderson had taken care to cut the phone wires, just in case.

He claimed he'd never intended to kill Elizabeth Lyman. However, when he entered the bedroom – close to midnight, he estimated – she'd woken up, and sat up sharply in her bed. Anderson was startled, he explained, so he raised his gun and shot around the dark room in a panic.

But the wound that killed Elizabeth Lyman wasn't consistent with Anderson's version of events. She died of a single bullet – from a .45 caliber – just underneath her left eye, determined to have been fired from a distance of approximately eight to twenty inches away.

After shooting the home's elderly occupant, Anderson said, he dug around and collected all the cash he could get his hands on – around $100. But then, instead of leaving the scene of the crime, he turned on the lights, pulled open the curtains, and cooked himself a little snack. He was still sitting there, watching television and eating his meal, when police showed up about three hours later.

Unfazed, Anderson confessed immediately – and also claimed responsibility for another six unsolved murders throughout Utah. He confessed that three years earlier, he had fatally stabbed another inmate named Robert Blundell, and had shot a number of people during a brief period where he'd hired himself out as a contract killer in the Las Vegas area.

"She didn't deserve that," Anderson later told the court. "I was very wrong."

"My lease is coming due."

The jury didn't deliberate for long before handing down a verdict. They found him guilty, and recommended the most severe penalty offered by the state. Anderson was to await his execution on death row at San Quentin, where he fell into a severe depression.

As the days passed, Anderson – who'd never had much opportunity to explore intellectual pursuits – began writing. He quickly amassed hundreds of poems, along with a number of novels and plays. He also learned that his IQ, which had tested at the "gifted" or "advanced" 136, put him a higher intellectual bracket than most of the population – particularly among those incarcerated in San Quentin.

It was especially impressive coming from the product of an abusive family situation who spent his teenage years living by himself, roaming the hills of New Mexico, after he'd been effectively disowned by his parents.

In 1998, when he was 45, Anderson composed a letter to a professor named Bell Gale Chevigny, who sat as chair for the prison program of the Poets, Essayists, and Novelists (PEN) American Center.

"I was passing through California when I shot someone during an $80 bungled burglary and found myself a permanent resident," his letter began. "That residency grows short; my lease is coming due."

His work impressed the professor, who eventually edited an anthology of prison writing called "Doing Time" which featured one of Anderson's pieces. His work also earned him two PEN awards – including the organization's top prize for poetry – and was even presented in an off-Broadway play called *Lament From Death Row*.

"(His work) struck me as very different to the stereotype of prison writing. At one point, he wrote to me that it was too bad he was only learning the meaning of life just as he was about to lose it," Chevigny wrote in a section of the anthology that discussed Anderson.

"He is a connoisseur of despair, the poet laureate of America's damned. He longs for an anthology of condemned prisoners' writings. His own gift of compassion may be the greatest reward for his personal transformation. In a recent poem, he wrote: 'Over these incarcerated years, I have heard men wail in the night, mourning misplaced lives and lost souls ... nothing seems as forlorn as the profound crying, of an unseen man weeping in solitude."

Chevigny came to believe that Anderson was not a murderer by nature – or, if he was, he was by this point completely rehabilitated. Other supporters – surprisingly – included the families of the two people he was known to have killed. Anderson himself had, however, recanted the murder confessions he'd made after his arrival at San

Quentin. His supporters claimed that he'd simply "made up all the hit man stuff."

In fact, such an explanation wouldn't have been all that far fetched. Fantasies are frequently a symptom of post traumatic stress disorder – a condition that likely could have impacted Anderson's life, considering the type of abuse he endured as a youth.

Court records detail the explanation Anderson provided the jury as to how he found himself headed down the wrong track as a youth. His mother, who had worked as a court clerk, had been falsely accused of embezzlement – and was soon after convicted and imprisoned. Although she was eventually released, when authorities discovered that the crime had actually been committed by the judge she'd worked for, she couldn't get past what she had suffered through.

"His mother never recovered from the trauma of this false conviction, and she died soon thereafter of cancer," court documents state. "Anderson testified that he was branded by schoolmates over this event, who taunted him with all sorts of derogatory names such as 'Tweety Bird' and 'Son of a Jail Bird.'"

According to Anderson's testimony, this event was a "cataclysmic episode" that fundamentally destroyed the way he saw the world and the justice system – which, ultimately, led him to seek out the "wrong crowd."

However, there was no arguing that – post traumatic stress disorder or not – Anderson had fatally shot Elizabeth Lyman. He'd also never denied the confession he'd made upon his arrest, when he took credit for the stabbing death of fellow inmate Robert Blundell at the Utah State Prison. According to court records, Anderson claimed he'd "had no use" for the man.

He claimed that the two had gotten into an argument in the prison's kitchen area over a reputation Blundell had earned for being a snitch. Blundell reacted by making a sexual threat at Anderson and then left the kitchen, "to get some milk for his coffee." Once Blundell's back was turned, Anderson grabbed a knife, went after Blundell, and plunged the weapon into his back.

In his own explanation to the authorities, Anderson said that he'd killed Blundell simply because "he got in my face at the wrong time and (probably) caught me in the wrong mood, you might say."

Another confession could not be confirmed by the police, however. Anderson took credit for a third homicide – a contract killing, which he said had been commissioned by a group of drug traffickers after he'd broken out of the Utah State Prison. He'd been paid $1,000 to shoot a man named Timothy Glashien, who he shot four times with the same gun he'd had in the botched robbery – the handgun that had killed Elizabeth Lyman.

There was insufficient evidence, at the time, to link Anderson to the crime; however, he had been named as a person of interest in the initial investigation.

"I'd just like to say that I did, I made these statements simply to clear up the fact that a lot of people were suspected of the crimes that shouldn't have been suspected," Anderson added, when detectives asked if he was making the statement on his own free will. "I had been informed of it by various people that it should be cleared up because they didn't have anything to do with it. And that's my main purpose here, with these crimes in Utah."

Still, his supporters argued that his thoughtful writings proved that no matter what Anderson had been responsible for doing in the past, he was obviously – now – a changed man.

"His poems showed that even the most brutalized person can rediscover who he or she is through imagination and thought," Chevigny wrote in one of the submissions she made to the state on Anderson's behalf.

A new defense team even tried to argue that the Lyman murder hadn't been planned out in advance. According to the prosecution, the murder of Elizabeth Lyman was a premeditated attack on an elderly victim who had been unable to defend herself. However, in Anderson's initial statement to the officers who arrested him, he claimed he had carefully staked out the property for two whole days before he finally broke in – seeing no sign of potential occupants, and no vehicle in the driveway, he said he'd believed that the home was vacant.

However, Elizabeth Lyman didn't own a car – as a non-driver, she had no need to. She'd been at the house the entire time, but hadn't gone outside or even opened her curtains. And, as Anderson searched the house for food and money, he came across the elderly homeowner. Startled by the encounter, he fired his gun in a panic – and a bullet connected with her face.

Anderson's supporters also alleged that he might not have been sentenced to death if it hadn't been for the "terrible job" done by his court-appointed attorney, Donald Ames. Two of Ames' other former clients had also received death sentences – which were eventually overturned, on the grounds of "incompetent representation."

Ames, who has since passed away, was referred to by one judge as "deceptive, untrustworthy and disloyal to his capital clients." The dissenting judge added that it was possible that the death penalty "may well have been imposed, not because of the crime that (Anderson) committed, but because of the incompetence of an attorney with little integrity and a pattern of ineffective performance in capital cases."

Even Ames' daughters had previously provided testimony against him. During an appeal in another, unrelated case, they asserted that he'd been both physically and psychologically abusive – and noted that he even frequently made comments of a racist nature with regards to some of his clients.

"This was a man who had no idea what was required to properly prepare for a capital case," said Donald Ayoob, one of the public defenders who worked on that separate case. "When it comes to the shoddy representation that capital defendants get at a trial, Don Ames was a poster boy."

However, a court ruling determined that Anderson had received an adequate defense in the trial, despite Ames' history of successfully arguing for death sentences that were later overturned. California Governor Gray Davis felt that, upon an extensive review of the evidence in Anderson's case, the conviction was correct – he was convinced that Anderson was guilty.

The death penalty hadn't even been sought by the victim's family, protestors pointed out. The relatives of both Elizabeth Lyman and Robert Blundell actively supported Anderson's bid for clemency, even – making legal history in California.

However, the many appeals and calls for clemency were unsuccessful, and after spending 22 years behind bars, Anderson's lease finally ran out on January 29, 2002.

The bard of the damned

The last-ditch battle for Anderson's life was lost just hours before he was pronounced dead of a lethal injection. By a vote of 8-0, the United States Supreme Court – minus the participation of Justice Antonin Scalia – rejected a request for a stay of execution on Anderson's case, and a request for a new hearing.

According to court documents, the prosecutor in Anderson's initial trial told the jury that Anderson was a "sociopath," who can't live with or "get along with" anyone else. The documents indicate that the State's case was "very powerful," and described in detail the various assaults, fights, and killings Anderson had been involved with prior to his final arrest.

"He kills people everywhere. He stabs people everywhere," he said in his opening argument. "There is no place that anybody is going to be safe from this individual. He looks out for old number one, and that's all he's concerned with. And forget about the rest of the world."

The prosecution alleged that Anderson was a "cold-blooded murderer who intentionally and wantonly killed a defenseless elderly woman" at close range, in her own home, for the purpose of eating her food and stealing her cash. However, the State argued that Lyman's murder was not a unique event – in fact, the prosecution claimed it was "just another violent act" in Anderson's "short but dangerous life," which kicked off with the armed robbery of a Farmington, New Mexico, school in 1971

According to the prosecution, this burglary at Farmington had involved Anderson pointing a rifle at two peace officers, threatening their lives. However, the defense argued that in that case, the officers had lied about the gun.

"He did have a rifle, but it was lying on the floor when they surprised him," Anderson's attorneys alleged. "He was never charged with, nor convicted of, pointing the rifle at the officers, only of the school burglary. In any event, no violence was involved in the incident – on that point, even the officers agreed."

Still, the prosecution's point had been made – Anderson did appear to have a propensity for aggressive behaviour. Other examples were presented to underscore this determination.

"Anderson's wanton violence continued even after he was incarcerated for the Farmington burglary, as evidenced by his conviction for aggravated assault with a knife on a fellow prisoner," the prosecution continued. "Undaunted by his conviction for stabbing one prisoner, he then knifed another prisoner, Blundell, to death on August 24, 1977. He then effectuated a successful walk-away escape from Utah State Prison, and shortly thereafter shot and killed Timothy Glashien for $1,000."

The prosecution also used Anderson's own words against him, claiming that at one point following his arrest, Anderson had told detectives, "I was born and trained to be a kiler. I always wanted to be a killer."

It was a strong enough argument to sway not only the jury and the Supreme Court, but also California Governor Gray Davis. Despite all the appeals filed and pleas for clemency presented to him, he remained unmoved – convinced of Anderson's guilt above all else.

"There is no dispute that Anderson, with an IQ of 136, is an extremely intelligent man," Davis said in a statement ruling out any possibility of Anderson's release. "But his intelligence, ironically, makes the brutality and indifference of his crimes all the more reprehensible."

"This was a totally unsought death in so many ways; both victims' families had said they did not want nor need the death penalty, and more than half the population of California opposes the penalty," Chevigny said in response. "The governor has ignored the will of his voters."

Anticipating this denial from Davis – the last time clemency was granted by a California governor was by Ronald Reagan, in 1967 – Anderson's defense team had also launched another legal battle. This time, his attorneys were arguing that by taking such a staunch, tough on crime position against crime, Davis had backed himself into a corner where clemency could never be granted – even filing an appeal the day before Anderson's execution, claiming Davis' opinion on Anderson's case clearly revealed the governor's bias.

Again, the team was unsuccessful. Anderson was sentenced to die.

"This was a part of his destiny."

The night of Anderson's execution, a vigil was held by hundreds of protestors and supporters – an Episcopal priest from Santa Cruz, Lyle Grosjean, was one of 15 individuals who had walked to San Quentin by foot all the way from San Francisco in an act of protest against capital punishment.

"We walk 25 miles to show our commitment that we're against the death penalty. Punishment isn't the answer – compassion is," he said. "We're unequivocally opposed to the death penalty in all cases, guilty or innocent."

Anderson himself remained eerily calm as he enjoyed yet another meal that would eventually make headlines. His last supper consisted of grilled cheese sandwiches, radishes, hominy and corn, cottage cheese, a pint of chocolate chip ice cream, and a slice of peach pie – at approximately 300 pounds, Anderson was certainly no stranger to dietary indulgences.

While other death row inmates spent their final hours talking about football, doing mundane chores like reading their mail, or spilling their deepest secrets, Anderson chose to end his life in the loneliest way.

"Periodically, he was asked if he wanted anything or anyone," said Bob Martinez, a spokesperson for the California Department of Corrections. "The answer was: 'Negative.'"

In the days leading up to his execution, Anderson stopped going outside. He gave away what few possessions he had left to other inmates at the prison. He asked that the guards turn away any spiritual advisors who showed up to talk with him – in fact, he refused to accept visitors of any kind, or even to come to the phone.

"Twenty years in here, I think it caught up with him," said Capt. K.J. Williams, who oversaw the more than 500 prisoners who sat on San Quentin's death row. "This was a part of his destiny. He accepted it."

At just 48 years of age, Anderson was brought into the death chamber of the San Quentin State Prison – painted a garish, hospital-like apple green – and his legs and arms were secured onto a padded gurney. There, he was injected with a lethal concoction of chemicals which began by rendering him unconscious before stopping his breath and, finally, his heart.

He'd been allowed to choose seven witnesses for the execution, but Anderson had designated only three – all valued members of his hard-working defense team. Typically, executions are attended by relatives of the victims; however, in Anderson's case, the families of the two people he was known to have killed had been clear in their belief that he did not deserve to be put to death for his crimes. They turned down the opportunity to witness it in person.

Approximately 40 people attended the execution – mainly law enforcement officers, journalists, and attorneys.

"He just completely withdrew," Williams said. "They all play tough. But after a while, you can tell it's getting to them. Not this guy – this was an unusual man. These people have done some terrible things, but they are still people. In a sense, this is the last dignity they have – to die with dignity. And he will do that."

He had no last words, even, until Margo Rocconi – one of his attorneys – mouthed the words, "I love you," through the glass. Silently, Anderson said, "Thank you."

With that, Anderson became the 10th man executed on California's death row, since capital punishment was reinstated in 1992 following a hiatus that lasted more than two decades.

Anderson had also declined the opportunity to make a final statement – according to what he told prison officials, the expansive collection of poetry and essays he'd penned during his years behind bars would speak for itself.

"Mr. Anderson was ... executed despite the fact that his life had redeeming value and that, as the poet laureate of the condemned, he still had so much more to contribute to the world," said the statement released by Anderson's legal team. "It has been a privilege to represent him. We will miss him greatly."

While his supporters continued to assert that Anderson "still had so much more to contribute to the world," evidence continued to mount even decades after his death to support the jury's original decision – that Stephen Wayne Anderson was a serial killer. Though, perhaps one with a sensitive way with words.

In fact, Utah police determined in June 2015 – 35 years later – that they had finally gathered sufficient evidence to link Anderson with another murder. This time, the bard of the damned was responsible for a contract killing, carried out execution style, because of a botched drug deal.

The victim, a 29 year old man named Timothy Glashien, had been shot four times, and according to the local police chief, Jim Winder, Anderson was initially a potential person of interest as the investigation got underway – and Anderson's possible involvement in the killing featured heavily in his trials. However, the detectives weren't able to be certain of the identity of Glashien's killer until new evidence was discovered when the cold case was reopened more than three decades later.

Still, there's no denying that – serial killer or not – Anderson had grown and changed over the course of his time in prison, and his five years on death row.

"The experience of being condemned to die made me grow up and realize that it was a serious matter," he testified. "And I matured. And I realized there's more to life than living the life that I had lived. And maybe I had a chance to change."

ANATOLY THE KILLER

WALLACE SCOTT

"I'm an angel who was attending a school of Satan. Some will call me schizophrenic or even Hitler or other terrible things. That's okay with me."
- Anatoly Onoprienko

CHAPTER ONE

Anatoly Onoprienko was born in the village of Lasky in Zhtomyr Oblast in the Ukraine on July 25th, 1959. His father, Yuri Onoprienko, was a World War II hero for the Soviet Union but according to Anatoly he was abusive and an alcoholic. He also had a younger brother who was thirteen years older than him.

His mother died when he was four years old and his father sent him to live with his grandparents and aunt. The grandparents subsequently sent him to an orphanage.

Onoprienko became bitter at his family and father for sending him to the orphanage. His older brother was allowed to stay in the family home while he was sent away.

"I remember my father and brother staring at me," Onoprienko said recalling his youth. "Staring at me saying, 'let's send him to an orphanage.' I don't blame them but I'm horrified by their memory. I remember their voices."

It is unknown why Anatoly was sent to the orphanage alone while his brother remained in the care of his father. His grandmother stayed with him for the first few days there, helping him to adjust. She would eventually leave but would visit often and bring care packages of food.

A shy and quiet young boy, he did manage to make friends inside the orphanage. He would play soccer and other sports. His grades began to decline, however, as he entered the college of forestry at age fourteen.

Teachers noted a shift in his personality and became concerned. He began drinking Vodka like his father and became involved in petty thefts.

Onoprienko left the college of forestry at the age of seventeen, still unsure of what to do with his life. He joined the army in 1976 and it is here where he mastered the use of firearms. Instead of becoming a good soldier, however, he became even more alienated.

"When I was twenty years old I called myself stupid because I couldn't understand people," Onoprienko recalled. "If they were smart then I must be stupid."

Onoprienko was discharged from the army then became a sailor. He gained employment on a cruise ship in Odessa and where he would often steal money from cabins. Despite his anti-social temperament, Onoprienko had a handful of girlfriends that he would try to impress with gifts purchased with money he had stolen.

One waitress on the cruise ship caught his eye and the two began dating. She would remain his girlfriend for three years and she would give birth to his first child. Onoprienko would take a stab at being a father for awhile but discovered that it wasn't for him.

Without a word, he left his girlfriend and his baby. Onoprienko would never see them again.

"I had a unique destiny," Onoprienko said. "I had to go out and find it. I felt restless at home. Stifled. Married life wasn't for me. I needed something more."

That "something more" would be crime and murder.

CHAPTER TWO

"Onoprienko's criminal activity would increase in 1989," Ruslan Moshkovsky (Onoprienko's attorney) said. "The USSR was collapsing and no one was responsible for anything."

Onoprienko's first murder would start with his landlady.

He broke into her apartment with the goal of stealing a few pieces of jewelry. The landlady, however, came home and demanded to know what he was doing in her house.

Onoprienko panicked and shot the woman dead.

He ran out of the apartment and continued on with his life as usual. Because the police resources were so stretched out, Onoprienko was never even questioned in the murder and the crime would remain unsolved.

Onoprienko would team up with a fellow petty thief, Sergei Rogozin, and the duo would break into various residences around Kiev.

Returning home from a night of thievery, the two spotted a car pulling a trailer late one night. Onoprienko sped in front of the vehicle, blocking its route then jumped out of his car with a sawed-off shotgun in hand.

A young couple was inside and Onoprienko fired upon them without warning.

"What are you doing?" Rogozin screamed.

"Shut up!"

"I thought we were just going to rob them."

Onoprienko sprang up in Rogozin's face, caressing his cheek with the barrel of his shotgun. "If you don't shut up...If you say anything, I will kill your entire family and make you watch. Do you understand?"

Rogozin could only nod his head in agreement.

Onoprienko then buried the bodies of the couple and set fire to their car.

A month later, the two thieves gunned down another couple using the same method. Onoprienko would speed in front of the car and stop. His victims caught unaware and defenseless, Onoprienko would spring out of his car and blast away.

Rogozin would say nothing and just take whatever valuables he could find off the victims.

Onoprienko would continue accumulating his victims in this manner. He would stop families on abandoned roads and kill everyone inside. Even children.

The home burglaries continued as well with Rogozin. Onoprienko killed a family of ten people when he and Rogozin were caught in the midst of robbing their house. Two adults and eight children were killed by the duo. Onoprienko then ceased all ties with Rogozin.

"He was a kind, intelligent man," Rogozin would say later of Onoprienko. "He wasn't greedy. He seemed good-natured. I cannot say anything bad about him."

CHAPTER THREE

Onoprienko kept a low profile for a few years, moving in with a distant cousin. There are six years in his life that are unaccounted for. Some say he spent some time in a mental institution while others insist that he may be responsible for more crimes in and around the former Soviet Union. He tried to get asylum in Western Europe but failed, returning to his native Ukraine.

"He worked in Germany and Austria," Dmitry Lipsky, the trial judge said. "During our interrogation we asked if he had killed anyone there. He denied it. He said he had only committed a robbery."

"At the very beginning, I had an option to commit suicide," Onoprienko said. "And to stop this mission to kill. But then with the passage of time there was an order from above that I cannot kill myself. I'm supposed to live and keep doing what I'm doing and finish this game."

Onoprienko would return to the Ukraine in 1985 and begin a killing rampage the likes of which his country had never seen. He had anticipated that his crimes on the highway would become the stuff of legend. Instead, they were forgotten in a bureaucratic quagmire.

Not only were his crimes unknown to the general public, no one was even investigating them.

The Soviet Union had collapsed and his native state, the Ukraine, was now an independent country.

"When he came back," Moshkovsky said. "And realized that everything had been forgotten and no one was looking for him, he embarked on his second killing spree."

Like a shark circling around a minnow of fish, Onoprienko moved from town to town surveying the lay of the land. He visited some relatives who were hunters and stole a shotgun from them.

Onoprienko would saw off the barrel of the gun in order to cause maximum damage. He wanted not only to kill again but to gain notoriety for the murders.

His new crime wave started with a seventy year old woman in Odessa. He broke into her home, shot her dead then set the home on fire.

"My main purpose wasn't to rob," Onoprienko said. "My purpose was cruel. I can't explain it. My purpose was to threaten people and threaten the police. And lead them in the wrong direction."

Days later, he would travel to a town called Malyn. He skulked around the town at night and come upon a young couple having sex in their car.

"I shot at them from the driver side," Onoprienko said. "I wounded the man then the woman jumped out of the car. I waited until she put her clothes on. Then she ran off. Probably to get some help."

The woman returned shortly thereafter to check on her lover. With Onoprienko hiding near the car, he stabbed her to death. He put the woman in the car, shot the man again then drove to a secluded area where he set the car on fire.

"I started realizing that there was a plan for me," Onoprienko said. "Something was giving me direction."

CHAPTER FOUR

Onoprienko began targeting families that lived in isolated areas around Kiev. He would follow the same modus operandi in each killing. He would create a distraction, usually throwing a brick through the front window to lure the adult male(s) out of the home. Then he would kill the man of the house before entering the home and killing the wife, saving the children for last. He would then set the house on fire in order to remove all evidence. There were instances wherein witnesses would cross his path and he would kill them as well.

Onoprienko was a nocturnal killer. During the day, he played the role of the down on his luck blue collar worker but at night he would seek out fame by being a serial killer.

He would move to a town called Yavoriv, moving in with a cousin named Pyotr and his wife Yelena. Ukrainian families were communal in nature and Pyotr saw it as his duty to take care of his struggling cousin.

Pyotr's wife Yelena, however, didn't like Onoprienko. She knew that there was something 'off' about the man and felt uneasy when she discovered the rifle under his bed.

Yelena pressured her husband into kicking Onoprienko out of the house. Pyotr could not throw his cousin out on the streets but he decided instead to play matchmaker. He knew a hair dresser that was recently divorced and looking for a decent man to be her meal ticket. Pyotor threw a family party, invite the woman over and she immediately hit it off with Onoprienko.

The woman was named Ana Kazak. She had two children of her own but her ex-husband was an alcoholic. She an attraction to the soft-spoken Onoprienko and the two began living together.

Onoprienko told his new live-in girlfriend that he was a "traveling businessman" and she never questioned his long absences from home.

Onoprienko would travel all the way to Malyn which was a town that was often hit by blackouts. He would be able to get in and out, do his killings under the cloak of night when no one had electricity nor did they have the capability to call for help. It was the perfect scenario for the serial killer.

CHAPTER FIVE

It was Christmas Eve when Onoprienko came upon the secluded home of the Zaichenko family which was located in the small village of Garmarnia. Inside, a forestry teacher lived along with his wife and two sons.

Onoprienko crept around the exterior of the home, found a ladder and propped it against the wall. He climbed up to the bedroom window and fired through the glass, killing the father and three year old son who was sleeping with him.

"I just shot them," Onoprienko said. "It's not that it gave me pleasure, but I felt this urge. From then on, it was almost like some game from outer space."

Onoprienko then jumped through the window and went from room to room.

"Don't kill us!" the wife pleaded as Onoprienko came through her door. He stabbed the woman and then strangled their three-month old baby.

"I didn't want to waste bullets on the weak," Onoprienko said.

He then ripped the wedding rings off the couple's hands as well as taking a small golden cross on a chain, earrings and clothes before torching the home.

Onoprienko would later say that he had "a vision from God" and was ordered to murder.

"When we arrived at the site, we were in shock," Leonid Martynenko, lead investigator of the Zaichenko murder said. "We discovered that the whole family had died violently. At the time, we didn't know the reason for the crime. We developed leads, examined a number of options. We considered burglary the main motive then. We thought it was homicide for purpose of robbery."

Onoprienko returned home and spent Christmas with Ana and her two sons. On New Year's Eve, however, the told her that he had to "go away on business."

Onoprienko would then travel to the town of Bratkovichi where he would indulge in his killing fantasies once again.

The streets of the town were deserted at night and Onoprienko was getting antsy. Then in the distance, he saw a man walking down the street.

"How you doing?" Onoprienko asked the man. "Was wondering if you could spare me a dollar or two so I can get something to eat?"

"Get the fuck away from me, you bum!" the man said. He was dressed in a forestry uniform and looked to be going home from work.

"Just a dollar."

"Fuck you!"

The man turned around and Onoprienko shot him in the back. The forester fell face first to the ground. Onoprienko quickly dragged the man to the side of the road. He rifled through his pockets, taking his money and keys. Then he stripped the man naked.

The night was just getting started for Onoprienko as he continued his rampage throughout the town. He noticed a man hanging curtains in his window and Onoprienko fired away, killing the man. Breaking into the home, he killed the man's wife and her twin sisters that were also living there. He then cut off the wife's finger and stole her wedding ring.

"It was like cutting through a tree branch," Onoprienko said. "It was very easy. Cutting through flesh was like cutting through butter."

He could not help but stop to admire his handiwork before he set the house ablaze.

"I was observing the victims," Onoprienko said. "Those who were already killed. How they were killed or were dying. Or how they were living the last minutes of their lives."

Onoprienko hopped on the train and returned home. When he got home, he took the wedding ring off the dead woman's finger and proposed to Ana.

"After the second murder we knew we had a maniac on our hands," Martynenko said. "We came to the location and viewed the scene. We saw the brutality of the crime and it had become absolutely clear to us that it was the same man that committed all the killings."

Gathering and sharing information still proved to be a problem in the Ukraine. Old Soviet style narratives were still being adhered to, like that of the government never admitting that serial killers existed in their country. It was part of the old Soviet style propaganda, wanting to prove to the world that killings didn't take place in their Communist territory. Even though the Ukraine was now free from such commandments, the leadership still adhered to keeping information away from the public and not admitting that they had a problem.

"It was striking how systematic the murders were," Romanyuk said. "There were group murders. Whole families were wiped out for no visible reason. That was really astounding."

Four days later after his marriage proposal, Onoprienko began gunning people down on the Berdyansk, Dnieprovskaya highway. He stopped cars, feigning as if he needed assistance then he would shoot the drivers. The victims were Kasai, a Navy ensign, a taxi driver named Savitsky, a kolkhoz cook named Kochergina and another unidentified victim.

"To me it was like hunting," Onoprienko said. "Hunting people down. I would be sitting, bored, with nothing to do. And then suddenly this idea would get into my head. I would do everything to get it out of my mind, but I couldn't. It was stronger than me. So I would get in the car or catch a train and go out to kill."

Onoprienko waited another eleven days, take a train to the village of Bratkovichi and invading the home of the Pilat family. He would shoot all five family members in the home and once again set fire to the place. He would be seen by two witnesses and he promptly killed them both.

"I look at it very simply," Onoprienko said. ""As an animal, I watched all this as an animal would stare at sheep."

The blood lust now running freely, Onoprienko could not refrain himself from killing.

On January 30th, 1996, Onoprienko killed a nurse named Marusina, her two sons and a family friend in Fastova, Kieskaya Oblast region of the Ukraine.

"I could not stop myself," he would say later to investigators. "I became obsessed with killing. To me killing people is like ripping up a duvet. Men, women, old people, children, they are all the same. I have never felt sorry for those I killed. No love, no hatred, just blind indifference. I don't see them as individuals, but just as masses."

Onoprienko would continue to take small items from the homes as souvenirs before going back home. He would bring his fiancee clothes, jewelry and a tape deck which he presented as gifts.

On February 19th , 1996, Onoprienko invaded the home of the Dubchak family. He shot and killed the father and son then bludgeoned the mother to death with a hammer. The family had a daughter, and he walked into her room to find her praying.

"Where do your parents keep the money!" he demanded.

The girl looked at her killer straight in the eye, defiant.

"Show me where the money is!"

"No, I won't," the girl said.

Onoprienko then killed the girl.

'That strength (the girl's) was incredible," Onoprieko said. "But I felt nothing."

Onoprienko then broke into the home of the Bodnarchuck family in Malina, Lvivskaya Oblast. He started with his usual tactic of throwing a rock at the door. The father, however, came out of the home with an ax. Onoprienko promptly shot the man and then the wife who came to the door to investigate the noise. Onoprienko then went inside and chopped up the daughters with the ax. A neighbor named Tsalk wandered onto the property and Onoprienko shot him to death before chopping up his body as well.

"Oh, you know, I killed them because I loved them so much," Onoprienko said. "Those children, those men and women, I had to kill them, the inner voice spoke inside my mind and heart and pushed me so hard!"

On March 22nd, 1996, Onoprienko shot and killed members of the Novosad family. He then set the house on fire to remove all traces of evidence.

"He would always set the places on fire," Romanyuk said. "People saw the fire and came to fight it. There was no evidence left only holes in the walls and cartridges."

Police would use forensic science to discover that the holes in the walls were left by a hunting weapon, specifically a gun that had the barrel sawed off.

"I'm not a maniac," Onoprienko said. "If I were, I would have thrown myself onto you and killed you right here. No, it's not that simple. I have been taken over by a higher force, something telepathic or cosmic, which drove me. I am like a rabbit in a laboratory. A part of an experiment to prove that man is capable of murdering and learning to live with his crimes. To show that I can cope, that I can stand anything, forget everything."

The Ukrainian government could no longer keep a lid on the killings. Rumors had spread of a man who was on a rampage throughout the entire country, murdering families at random.

The people of the region all lived in fear. Some families would stay together at night and press their furniture up against the door at night.

"People would come home from work early," said one Ukrainian resident. "People were scared to death. Students who were away at college quickly came home to be with their parents. I had one neighbor that put bars on their windows. Everyone was scared."

The press had given him the nickname of "The Terminator."

Onoprienko had achieved his goal. He had become the most feared man in his country.

CHAPTER SIX

The Ukrainian military patrolled certain villages to keep the people safe. Schools near the murders were shut down as a precaution. There was daily radio updates and a lot of the citizens likened the experience to being in a war.

"All the police departments were given specific instructions as to what to look for," Romanyuk said. "They knew how the killer behaved, that he acted at night. They investigated any sound. Even when a dog barked at night. The orders were strict."

The Ukraine launched a sweeping manhunt, determined to find the killer. They were convinced that this was the work of one man and dispensed their National Guard plus over 2,000 police investigators on the case.

"We had special teams of different officers working in different capacities," Bodgan Romanyuk, the chief of police said. "We had officers in the field, around-the-clock gathering information and working with operatives. Then there were others who in charge of strategy, who conducted the ground operations."

Later that month, the Security Service of Ukraine (SBU) and the Public Prosecutor's Office specialists arrested a 26-year old man named Yury Mozola, thinking he was responsible for the family murders. Over the course of three days, seven Ukrainian law enforcement officials tortured the young man, employing burning, electrocution and beatings.

Mozola, however, refused to confess and would later die during the torture.

The seven men were then prosecuted for the murder and sentenced to jail.

Days later after Mozola's death, Onoprienko was finally captured after a massive manhunt.

An anonymous caller gave police a tip on Onoprienko. He said that he witnessed him trying to conceal a shotgun as he left his apartment building.

Police then surrounded Onoprienko's building, staking out every possible exit until storming the apartment.

"It was quite risky," Romanyuk said. "Because on the one hand there was no evidence. But, on the other hand, what if it's him? What if it is this trained killer who shoots people dead on the spot and our officers are only human."

"We had learned that our suspect was anti-social. He wouldn't open the door to anyone. It was Easter and his fiance went to visit her mother, out of town. She would return in the evening and when we rang we'd hope that he'd think that it was her coming home."

The police came to the door and knocked.

Opening the door was a small man with red hair.

He opened the door calmly, expecting his girlfriend.

The police forced their way in and demanded his identification.

Onoprienko then reached for his gun but the police overpowered him, grabbing his wrists. Wresting the pistol away, they identified it as one that had been stolen from a crime scene.

Searching the man for his identification, they recognized him as Anatoly Onoprienko.

"In the apartment is everything," Romanyuk said. "All the evidence is there. Things from the crime scenes where he murdered people in different regions."

The police officers held up the numerous guns and knives to his face.

"It isn't mine!" the killer protested. "All that stuff doesn't belong to me."

His fiancee Ana, return home. She was shocked to see Onoprienko being arrested as she maintained that he had been the sweetest man she had ever met and had been nothing but nice to her and her two children.

The police, however, disputed her notions by showing her the weapons that he had stashed in her apartment.

"I started talking with his fiancee," Romanyuk recalled. "And I tried to find ways of connecting him with these murders. We were able to match dates. She would give us a date when he wasn't home for a day or two and that date would correspond with the murders."

The police searched through the apartment and found over one-hundred twenty-two items that were taken from the crime scenes. Guns and knives all matched what they were looking for in terms of murder weapons.

After the debacle with the previous suspect, the police authorities wanted proof beyond a shadow of a doubt.

"For me," Romanyuk said. "It was crucial that it we were sure that it was him. To make sure that he could be tied to these killings."

The police brought the killer into the station and interrogated him until six o'clock in the morning. Onoprienko denied all involvement until he finally cracked early in the morning.

"I was commanded by God to kill," Onoprienko told his interrogators. "I was chosen because I'm a superior specimen. I have the power of hypnosis and can call animals through telepathy. I can stop and start my heart with my mind."

He told of being diagnosed with schizophrenia and being admitted to a hospital in Kiev.

"He told us about all fifty-two murders he committed," Romanyuk said. "Not only the ones he performed in 1995 but also about the murders he committed in the past a long time ago."

Onoprienko expressed relief at being caught. He had grew tired of killing and being covered in blood all the time.

The police then turned Onoprienko over to the Ukrainian interior ministry.

Upon his transference to this higher authority, Onoprienko immediately began making demands.

"Give me a box of candy," Onoprienko said. "Sausages and some crackers. Otherwise I won't talk to you."

Onoprienko was then allowed to take advantage of a strange quirk in Ukrainian law. In the Ukraine, a trial cannot commence until the defendant has read all of the evidence against him.

At his leisure.

Onoprienko was obligated to read over volumes of police reports and crime scene photos. There were over fifty-two dead bodies, some dismembered and burned. Finally, he relented and after seven months he led the police to the areas where he had killed his victims. Onoprienko would detail each murder with an eery calmness, remarking at how easy it was for him to kill his victims.

There was another delay in that the Ukraine would have to transport, feed and house all of the witnesses who came from different parts of the country. Ultimately, there would be no witnesses testifying at his trial as some of the family members did not want to come forth.

A full three years after his apprehension, Onoprienko was finally brought to trial. Onoprienko was forced to sit in court in an iron cage. People spat upon him and threatened to tear him apart.

"I'm a person, a regular person," Onoprienko said. "Anybody can become a murderer. I was helped. It either it a God or the devil. Whatever he calls himself."

"He needs to be shot!" screamed a woman in the court room.

"He does not deserve to be shot!" screamed another. "He needs to die a slow and agonizing death."

The trial drew national publicity and the security around the courtroom was tight.

Judge Dmytro Lypsky asked Onoprienko if he had anything to say.

"No, nothing," the killer said shrugging his shoulders.

"You have been informed of our legal rights-"

"It's your law," he growled.

"State your nationality," the judge said.

"None."

"That's impossible."

"According to the police," Onoprienko said. "I'm Ukrainian."

"Do you have anything else to say in your defense?"

"I've been a robot for years," the killer said. "Driven by dark forces. I should not be put on trial until authorities can determine the force. You are not able to take me as I am. You do not see all the good I'm going to do! And you will never understand me. This is a great force that controls this hall as well. You will never understand this. Maybe only your grandchildren will understand.

Onoprienko was cooperative throughout the trial until the end. He requested that his state-appointed lawyer, Ruslan Mashkovsky, be replaced by someone who was "at least 50 years old, Jewish or half-Jewish, economically independent and has international experience."

The court refused his request. He was confined to a metal cage inside the courtroom as the rest of the proceedings took place.

"I started preparing for prison life a long time ago," Onoprienko recalled. "I fasted, did yoga, I am not afraid of death," Onoprienko said. "Death for me is nothing. Naturally, I would prefer the death penalty. I have absolutely no interest in relations with people. I have betrayed them. The first time I killed, I shot down a deer in the woods. I was in my early twenties and I recall feeling very upset when I saw it dead. I couldn't explain why I had done it and I felt sorry for it. I never had that feeling again."

The closing arguments began in April of 1999. Prosecutor Yury Ignatenko pressed for the death sentence while Moshkovsky would try to bring up Onoprienko's childhood to generate his sympathy.

"My defendant was deprived of motherly love since the age of four," Moshkovsky argued. "And the absence of care which is necessary for the formation of a real man. I appeal to the court to soften the punishment."

Moshkovsky himself, however, knew that Onoprienko was the epitome of evil, saying and doing things for dramatic effect.

"He was a cunning, shrewd and a great psychologist," Moshkovsky said later. "He was hard to catch because he acted alone and without accomplices. He was a butcher, killing defenseless and poor people. He specifically chose villages on the outskirts where there was no telephone, where even cars pass with difficulty. Even if someone heard a shot, there would be no one to call."

After only three hours of deliberation, the judge sentenced Onoprienko to death by shooting.

"I've robbed and killed," Onoprienko said in his final statement. "But I'm a robot, I don't feel anything. I've been close to death so many times that it's even interesting for me now to venture into the after world, to see what is there, after this death."

The Ukraine, however, had just joined the Council of Europe and had committed to abolishing capital punishment.

Onoprienko was then spared the death penalty even though he gave the President of the Ukraine a personalized letter that he would kill again.

"If I am ever let out, I will start killing again," Onoprienko wrote. "But this time it will be worse, ten times worse. The urge is there. Seize this chance because I am being groomed to serve Satan. After what I have learnt out there, I have no competitors in my field. And if I am not killed I will escape from this jail and the first thing I'll do is find Kuchma (the Ukrainian president) and hang him from a tree by his testicles."

The Terminator would die of heart failure in the prison of Zhytomyr on August 27th, 2013 at the age of 54.

MANIAC

FRANK COLEMAN

Alexander Pichushkin - the Bitsa Park Maniac

*Stranger than **Fiction***

In 2010, journalist Denis Faye sat down with industry expert Pat Brown in an attempt to bridge the gap between how serial killers are portrayed in film and television and how they are in real life. Brown quickly cuts through the existing information floating around on this disparity.

> *"Faye: So what does Hollywood get right about serial killers?*
> *Brown: Very little."*

In the case of "real life" serial killer Alexander Pichushkin, known as the infamous Bitsa Maniac, the Chessboard Killer, and arguably one of Russia's most consummate serial killer, it's almost impossible to draw the line between fact and fiction. Between his mysterious past, the inventiveness of the press, and his own fabrications, Pichushkin's story requires an eye for the difference between killers from the silver screen and true monsters.

Described as a "real-life criminal profiler," Pat Brown has a lot to say about the difference between the fictional serial killers we see in movies and television and the all too real murderers we catch glimpses of in the news. In an interview with the WGA, she attempted to outline some of the most prominent errors writers make when depicting serial killers. She immediately honed in on the false complexity that writers default to in order to create drama, lamenting that such specificity is almost never the case.

> *"They're not as bizarre as the films show... [They] tend to over-profile the killer's mental state."*

In the news, Alexander Pichushkin's story has been sensationalized and stretched, the gaps in his narrative filled with fiction. Between

1992 and 2006 Pichushkin was responsible for the deaths of up to 62 people, putting him in the running for being one of Russia's most prolific serial killers. But despite this infamy and attention, there are plenty of holes in the account of his killing spree for reporters to expound and invent. Even Pichushkin's Wikipedia entry contains an entirely fictional tale of his childhood inspired solely by his title as the Chessboard Killer. This moniker may be the most popular and certainly most evocative option for Pichushkin, but it is by no means the most accurate. Those who were most affected by this slew of murders and know the most about them, locals and experts alike, all prefer the more succinct and accurate name Pichushkin had earned: the Maniac.

Creating a **Monster**

Psychologists often argue whether the monstrousness of serial killers is born or made by trauma or environment. On one hand, being able to point a finger at exactly what caused a human being to do such horrible things can be comforting, but all too often external factors are used to distance killers from blame and evoke sympathy. Brown laments that this distancing is what she is most opposed to in the portrayal of serial killers. "I've never seen a serial killer with redeeming qualities or one you can have some kind of sympathy for, like it's just a bad hobby he's got." On the other hand, a world with the potential for people who are simply born to commit heinous murders is a scary one to imagine, and given the number of environmental similarities between serial killers, one that frankly doesn't seem to exist.

Currently, the prevailing argument is that it is a combination of the natural and nurtured elements of someone's personality that react upon one another to create a psychopath, though Brown feels there is more of a conscious choice involved. "He's just pissed off at society and became a psychopath when life didn't work out his way..." In the case of Pichushkin, close analysis of his childhood, family, and early social interactions reveal many of the trademarks common in other serial killers, however, Brown's reminder of free will is an important one to keep in mind. While Pichushkin's childhood has some traumatic roots, ultimately he was not *made* into a monster—he *chose* to commit murder, and on a minimum of 52 separate occasions.

On April 9th, 1974 Alexander Pichushkin was born in Mytishchi, Moscow, and according to his mother, Natasha Pichushkina, he was a normal child as far as she could tell. Alexander, or Sasha for short, lived in a modest one bedroom apartment with his father and mother who had grown up in that same apartment. The complex is one of many on the outskirts of Moscow, a decaying remainder of soviet era infrastructure and some of the only reasonably priced housing in the area. Nicknamed *khrushchevki* after Nikita Khrushchev, the spartan public housing lacks charm and personality, but continues to serve in functionality and affordability. A mere nine months after Sasha is born, his father leaves Natasha to raise their son alone.

> *"I tried to raise him like a normal mother... I know now that I raised my son very poorly... [but] I can't say what I did wrong."*

Besides his mother's account in a popular interview from 2007, not much is known about young Sasha's childhood. One of the few verified details of Sasha's childhood is the head trauma he incurred at the age of four when he fell backward off a swing outside the *khrushchevki* only for it to swing toward him again and strike his forehead. Immediately following the incident he spent time in an institution for the disabled, though exactly how long he stayed there is not reported. Brain injuries, specifically to the frontal lobe where Sasha was struck, are very common among serial killers. David Berkowitz, Leonard Lake, Kenneth Bianchi, and John Gacy all suffered similar head trauma early in life, which neuroscientists link to violence and impulse control issues, as well as emotional and empathetic difficulties.

There are plenty of other mixed and unsubstantiated accounts of torment in Sasha's childhood inflicted by bullies instead of by accident, including one anecdote about a group of children ganging up on Sasha to steal his moped. A police investigator offered a possible explanation in an interview, saying that "Pichushkin" is a name with an effeminate, weak connotation, a detail that would otherwise be lost to the cultural barrier. Entrenched in a Russian cultural context often tinged with homophobia and toxic ideas of masculinity, young Sasha had his cards stacked against him. With the effeminate name, an absent father, a stint in an institution, and very few, if any, friends, he was ideal fodder for grade school bullies. Despite Pichushkin eventually outgrowing his childhood weaknesses and becoming a model image of Russian masculinity, many experts speculate that he might not be heterosexual.

Mentioned only briefly in an interview with the lead investigator, the question of the Bitsa Maniac's sexuality was quickly brushed off. Pichushkin smoked and drank, had a menial physical job stocking shelves at a grocery store, and a low voice with a gruff personality—to those surrounded by the cultural context of Russia's now-infamous homophobia, there was no possible way he could be anything but straight. Add in the brutal success of his murderous impulses and there is no hope of swaying the investigation's narrow image of Pichushkin.

His mother Natasha brought up in her 2007 interview that he never seemed to be interested in women or sex in general. His only documented emotional attachment is to a male classmate from his teens. An overwhelming majority of his victims, the people he was able to lure most easily and was most comfortable with, are all male ranging from as young as nine years old to retirement age. While there was never evidence of any sexual assault on his male victims to substantiate any of these claims, there also was a complete lack of sexual activity with his female victims as well. Based on the available, though sparse, information, it seems just as likely that Sasha lacked sexual impulse at all, and instead only had a lust to kill.

Yet another facet in the claims against Pichushkin's heterosexuality, young Sasha seemed to be heavily influenced by another serial killer, Andrei Chikatilo, whom he idolized to the extreme. Chikatilo's crimes came to light just as Sasha reached his most consciously formative years, and he kept careful track of his contemporary's every move. Chikatilo's spree of murders earned him the nickname of the Rostov Ripper, but he, like Sasha, was deemed by the press a maniac.

Finding *Inspiration*

In December of 1991 the newly liberated Russian media received news of an arrest made in relation to the series of unsolved, gruesome murders happening 117 miles northeast of Moscow, in Rostov von don. For nearly a decade the area had been terrorized by murders that were clearly linked to the same killer, who had been referred to as the Rostov Ripper. Immediately after the arrest, sensationalist news sources had yet to learn his name or see his photo, but had a brief summary of his crimes. His signature was stabbing, usually in excess of 30 times, gouging of the eyes, sexual assault, and evisceration; accused of 53 counts of murder in this style, the man whose name would later be learned became simply *the Maniac*. The public did not lay eyes upon the monster that they knew so little about until he appeared at the first day of his trial on April 14th the following year.

Just five days after Sasha's eighteenth birthday the media is suddenly saturated with the face of the Rostov Ripper, now revealed to be Andrei Chikatilo. His sallow face is pictured from behind iron bars throughout the trial, specially put in place of the usual plexiglass box, to protect him from the often hysterical and retaliatory relatives of his victims. These attacks were not the only noteworthy outbursts of the trial: Chikatilo and the judge, Leonid Akubzhanov, remained combative toward each other throughout the proceedings, with

Chikatilo refusing to cooperate. Ignoring questions posed by the prosecution, Chikatilo's original well-spoken demeanor devolved into a show-stopping display of chaos, singing socialist anthems and exposing himself to the jury in an attempt to be deemed unfit to stand trial.

As the trial continued into the summer, news outlets revealed more of Chikatilo's gory past, full of sexual assault while in his teaching position, torturous excess during his killings, and the numerous occasions he was apprehended, questioned, or suspected before his final arrest. Sasha followed all of these stories with more than the morbid curiosity typical of a boy his age. He clipped articles from the papers and kept photos of Chikatilo's face, images with captions that described him as a "shaven-skulled demon" and articles detailing the horrific, decade long murder spree of *the Maniac*.

With the clarity of hindsight, Pichushkin's serial murders appear to be somewhat spawned from Chikatilo's, if not directly inspired. Teenaged Sasha was exposed to widespread press coverage of his killings and saw the attention he garnered from the public and his victims' families. He witnessed the controversy over Chikatilo's punishment, which arguably contributed to the suspension of Russia's death penalty in 1996 (notably, after executing yet another serial killer, Sergey Golovkin). At the very least, Pichushkin seemed intent on surpassing Chikatilo in number, keeping track of his alleged 61 victims with numbers pasted on his now-infamous chessboard. While journalists after the fact like to fixate on this chessboard and invent a final goal of filling it with 64 murders, Pichushkin never mentioned the board in his taped confession. Motivated only by his need to kill and desire to overshadow the Rostov Ripper, the lead police investigator doubted Pichushkin would stop when he ran out of squares.

"Pichushkin is quite an unusual serial killer he's a hunter, a typical hunter and his only motivation was to kill, there was no other motive, whatever else we might have thought."

*A New **Maniac** Begins*

On the 27th of July, Sasha takes his first step towards becoming the infamous Bitsa Maniac. Now three months after turning eighteen years old, he invites his friend and classmate Mikhail Odichuck to join him in something he has been ruminating possibly for years: to commit his first murder. For Pichushkin, this is the most intimate gesture he could possibly offer. Only a trusted friend, a confidante, someone he would deem worthy of sharing such a powerful experience of control and subversion of societal expectations could have been welcomed so wholly into Sasha's inner circle. Unfortunately for both boys, what Sasha viewed as a generous offer, Mikhail saw as a joke.

It would be easy to jump to the conclusion that Sasha held some form of fondness or affection towards his classmate Mikhail. With the seeming absence of his sexual attraction to women in combination with idolization of Chikatilo and experience being bullied as a child, their relationship could have even been interpreted as a boyhood crush. Out of 51 charges of murder and attempted murder, only three victims were female, a statistic that belies Pichushkin's gravitation toward men in general. At such an important developmental stage in his life, Sasha would be expected to display sexual and emotional attraction towards those he felt closest to at the time, namely his friend Mikhail. With over a decade of experience in examining the personalities of serial killers, specialist Pat Brown would insist otherwise.

> *"What people don't get is that a psychopath can portray, at certain points in his life, certain levels of affection... [but] those are just objects in his life... People are either useful, or they're in the way."*

Mikhail made the mistake of getting in the way. Eventually the boy realized Sasha was dedicated to the idea of murder—and completely prepared. He knew to prey on the elderly and the homeless, strangers, who wouldn't be missed by family or valued by the police enough to warrant further investigation. He had already crafted the story of his "beloved" dog's grave in Bitsa Park as a trick to lure their victims with promise of a free drink, both lowering their victim's guard and impeding their ability to fight back. Most importantly, Sasha had discovered the manholes in Bitsa Park that fell up to 18 meters deep, full of highly pressurized currents, in which he would later dispose of twenty to thirty bodies. At exactly what point Mikhail came to the realization that Sasha was deadly serious, only Pichushkin knows—but his classmate never made it to the forest. That Monday afternoon Mikhail's lifeless body is found in the street, after dropping from a five-story balcony. Young Sasha was questioned by police, but they never suspected his involvement and ruled the tragedy a suicide with little to no other inquiry.

Prompted by Pichushkin's confession fifteen years later, a follow-up investigation examined Mikhail's body and discovered head trauma that didn't fit within expectations of impact on the ground. What they had glossed over appeared to be evidence that 18 year old Sasha had bashed in his classmate's head up to 21 times with an unidentifiable blunt object before lifting his lifeless body over the edge of the balcony to drop into the street below. Though the final result is similar to the neat, premeditated M.O. he would adopt later in life, this first murder was a crime of passion, fueled by betrayal and rage, and a moment Pichushkin would later look back on fondly.

"This first murder," he began in his televised confession, "It's like first love—It's unforgettable."

An Experimental Phase

For the next nine years, Pichushkin waits. Investigators speculated that Sasha repressed his homicidal urges for as long as possible, knowing that he would not be able to stop once he started again. Pichushkin neither confirmed nor denied these claims, and has offered no other explanation for such a long hiatus. But after those nine years are up, Sasha embarks on a personal journey with an astonishing body count, to discover all the ways he can kill and all the ways he can get away with it.

Now at the age of 27, Sasha began to mix up his M.O., experimenting with weapons, victims, and body disposal. The homeless were his first choice of victims, on whom he tested out another toss over the balcony and a homemade "pen shooter" Sasha had crafted himself; Pichushkin lamented in an interview that both of these methods were over too quickly. This second falling victim was only nine years old, whose death was overlooked just like Mikhail's. As for the pen shooter incident, Pichushkin later described the murder in his confession with explicit detail, from finding a homeless man sleeping on the street, to pressing the makeshift gun to his temple in broad daylight and watching him bleed. He explained that he had seen the man as an opportunity while he was walking to work and couldn't resist.

Eventually he moved on to victims who needed to be lured into the cover of the park, but these still would not be the bodies found by police and attributed to the Bitsa Maniac. The story Sasha told many of his victims centered on a "beloved" deceased dog, whose grave, he told them, was in the park. He would offer a drink of vodka over the nonexistent burial site to distract and relax them; little did they know that the spot he lead them to was strategically located by one of the manholes he had discovered in his youth. Sasha would then bash their heads on the manhole cover, only to open it and lift their inebriated or even unconscious bodies over the edge. His story varied slightly each time, and he continued to use opportunities like the sleeping homeless man to take advantage of poor drunks who wouldn't be missed amid his more focused strategy. Yet another distinction between fact and fiction, where news outlets attempted to fit all of Pichushkin's murders into a neat little box, Brown argues that just isn't so.

"[A real serial killer] doesn't have a fantastic signature with every crime, something really creepy that links every one of the crimes together ... It's very exciting, but it's not the way it is in real life. He's not always going to use the same method. He might try something else on another day, so you have to be careful of that."

When he later told police of his use of the sewer system to dispose of the corpses, they tested its validity by dropping a mannequin inside, only for it to be immediately torn apart by the forceful currents. They also later found the body of a missing person whose death Pichushkin had claimed fault of further into the system. Pichushkin blamed the police force's ineptitude for not being able to find the bodies he had so effectively destroyed. Normally the police would have to rely on what little evidence they have to corroborate a murderer's often fantastical claims and any particulars are reliant on the trustworthiness of a murderer. In Pichushkin's case, his haste to kill left three survivors in his wake who told police and the press every minute detail.

The first to live to tell the tale was Maria Viricheva, who was pregnant at the time of her attempted murder. Pichushkin met her in a metro station on February 23rd 2002 and must have been able to recognize that she was in pressing financial need. He crafted a story of cameras he had hidden away in a manhole in Bitsa Park, offering to sell them to her at a discount so she might turn a profit. Desperate, Maria accepted and followed him into the forest. At the opening to the sewer, Maria quickly realized her mistake as Pichushkin grabbed her and beat her head against the lid, which he then opened and dropped her inside. Miraculously, Maria maintained consciousness, and gripped the slippery walls while attempting to regain some strength amidst the freezing currents. Maria estimated that she spent almost 20 hours trapped in the sewer, struggling between trying to find a way to climb out and her fading will to live. Eventually she discovered rungs that lead to another manhole and was able to climb out to safety.

In addition to Maria, 13 year old Mikhail Lobov fell victim to Pichushkin's invitation to the park for a free drink and cigarettes. Mikhail was just one of many in a crowd of leather jackets and piercings, often hanging around the metro stations, loitering in front of food stands, and drinking. Investigators were unable to find any footage of Mikhail and Pichushkin together in the metro station nearest Bitsa Park, but they still speculate that the most likely place they met would be there. Once in the park, Mikhail's story reads like just like the others—an offer of vodka over the imaginary dog's grave, head meets manhole cover, and into the sewer he goes. The exception to the normal script comes when Mikhail's leather jacket catches on a piece of metal rather high up in the sewer, and his fall is stopped before he even reaches the water. Completely unaware, Pichushkin leaves the park thinking he killed the boy. Just moments later, Mikhail is able to crawl out shaken and disturbed, but with only minor head injuries.

Possibly the most unsettling part of these survivors' stories is when they turn to the local police to report their attacker, only to be turned away. Hospitalized and having just received news that she lost her pregnancy, Maria Viricheva frantically described the entire ordeal from beginning to end, including a full description of Pichushkin's appearance. Instead of taking action, police ignored her account and instead asked for her citizenship documentation. Maria didn't have any, and the police generously offerto ignore the whole situation, leaving her injured and alone in a hospital with Pichushkin continuing his murder spree.

When Mikhail went to police, they brushed him off as a lying punk and told him to go home. Not a month later, Mikhail ran into Pichushkin in a crowded metro station and began yelling and pulling at his hair in frustration, dragging his attacker over to a policeman standing guard and demanding vindication. The officer escorted

Mikhail out of the station and told him again just to go home. Possibly even worse is the third survivor case, of a middle aged homeless man whose story has continued to be ignored and undocumented, even in the wake of Pichushkin's conviction.

Corroborated by these detailed survivor accounts, Pichushkin's confession weaves in the rest of the story. While the sewer was serving him well for body disposal, he still wasn't getting the satisfaction he was looking for. Instead of simply using the manhole cover, Sasha escalated to bringing a yellow-handled utility hammer with him to bash in the skulls of his victims before throwing them in the sewer. At this point, around thirty people had gone missing from his neighborhood. Police still weren't interested in the goings-on of the lower class, but the local gossip had begun to gain footing and Sasha wanted credit for his work.

*The Hunt for the **Bitsa Maniac***

It's not until August 15th, 2005 that the police discover their first body, deep in Bittsevsky Park. The victim was a 31 year old man named Nikolai Wirogiev, who had suffered extensive head trauma and, most shockingly, had a vodka bottle lodged in the wound. Law enforcement officer Denis Adamenko was one of the first on the scene; years later he is still able to pinpoint the exact place the first body was found, and describe the scene with gruesome detail. Though he had no idea what was in store at the time of the first police-documented murder, Adamenko would continue working on the case from the first body to Pichushkin's trial.

One month later, another man with the same injuries is found in the park. Just two weeks after that yet another body is found, and then again after only one week. Very suddenly the police began to link the murders together, realizing these stranger killings had to be the handiwork of a single killer. Though the vodka bottle signature isn't present every time, bodies begin piling up within the same age range and sex, all with substantial brain injuries. Sometimes in lieu of a vodka bottle, sticks are found in the wounds, but the reasoning for their presence remains the same: Sasha now likes to play with his victims after the fact.

Brown's interview offers some further insight into Pichushkin's newest escalation, explaining that the often-overlooked element of power is usually what creates specific signatures, such as the vodka bottle or sticks, instead of overly complex motives. "It's just that the fun ends too quickly, so instead of walking away from the body, they want to play with it because they can continue having control. *Now I'm eating you! Look at that!* It's an ongoing feeling of power."

In November of 2005 the police receive a wake up call in the form of the brutalized body and fifth victim of the unknown serial killer, a man named Nikolai Zakharchenko who was a 63 year old pensioner and an ex-cop. Like many of Pichushkin's victims, Zakharchenko lived in the same *khrushchevki* with his family, just two doors down from his murderer. Up until this point, every victim had been part of the underprivileged lower class, either homeless without family or deemed low priority by biased police. Claiming Pichushkin consciously targeted members of society that would not be missed or investigated, as some news sources allege, would be giving him far too much credit. An opportunist at heart, Sasha simply killed whenever he had the chance, with no regard for background or lack thereof, leading to the critical mistake of killing the former policeman. It's only at this point that police give the case with an accumulating body count over to an elite murder squad within the force. What the investigators don't know is that the fifth body that they've found is actually the 41st murder Sasha would later be convicted of.

By the beginning of the next year, news of a serial killer in Moscow had been upgraded from rumors among the working class to front page news. Reports from the Moscow Times warned residents of murders in

Bittsevsky Park, introducing the nickname 'Bitsa Maniac' for the first time. Pichushkin's half sister Katya, who lived in the same apartment as Sasha with her husband and child, later discussed in an interview seeing a news reel about the Maniac on tv and panicking for her brother's safety. It was well known that Sasha frequented the park, but she recalls he was never afraid that there was a killer on the loose. Meanwhile, the body count continued to rise.

A **Red Herring** in Bitsa Park

In a fit of desperation, both the police and the general public began speculating wildly about the killer's possible identity. The investigation's gaze soon turned to the sanitarium looming suggestively on the edge of Bitsa Park. Many of the patients at the ward had privileges that included the freedom to leave the building during the day without aid, and police could not help but notice that the dumping grounds fell well within walking distance. Officers immediately restricted this freedom pending further inquiry; what began as a series of interviews eventually escalated into the interrogation of every single patient with the means to walk to the park. Eventually this branch of the investigation ceased, producing no leads or valid suspects.

By mid-February, a series of sensational rumors arose fueled purely by the area's vicious homophobia. Whispers citing evidence that never existed and eyewitness accounts simply looking for their five minutes of fame circulated not from the humble residents of the *khrushchevki,* but from the panicked upper middle class. Suddenly past visitors to the park came out of the woodwork, claiming they saw the killer fleeing through the trees and describing him as a man in women's clothing and a wig. Yet another piece of gossip spread claiming some of the bodies had been raped and found with lipstick marks all over the face, neck, and body.

Demonstrating they are not immune to the rampant homophobia and transphobia of the people they protect, local police claimed an innocent victim to their witch hunt. Late at night on February 20th, someone whom the lead investigator later described as a middle aged transvestite was seen in Bitsa Park by police canvassing the area and whose mere presence was immediately deemed suspicious.

Accounts of what followed vary greatly, with many sources glossing over the resulting exchange entirely. Claims range from the suspect attempting to flee, mysteriously breaking free of handcuffs, to pulling a knife that was never found and threatening the policemen directly. One source described nearly 200 officers being called to the scene to detain this one person. The most agreed upon and substantiated elements of that night seem to be that the suspect had a hammer in their bag, and one thing led to another that resulted in police shooting the suspect in the leg and requiring hospitalization. It was later found that their "suspect" had corroborated, air-tight alibis for each of the murders and had done nothing wrong; the hammer had been for protection against the Maniac.

*Apprehending the **Culprit***

Two months and nine bodies later, the police finally caught their break in the form of Marina Moskalyeva, the first victim since young Mikhail with direct ties to Pichushkin. Marina was a single mother to her 15 year old son and worked full time at the same grocery store as Sasha. Not only had they worked together, but when questioned after the fact, Marina's son described Pichushkin as her boyfriend and had met him before. Thanks to a subway ticket in the pocket of her jacket, police were able to easily find footage of Pichushkin meeting Marina at a metro station just outside Bitsa Park on the day of her murder. In case that had not been enough, Marina had left a note with her son saying she was going for a walk in the park, naming Sasha Pichushkin and even listing his phone number in case her son needed her.

Marina had known there was a killer at large in Bitsa Park and went anyway; likewise, Pichushkin knew Marina had left a note with his name and number, and still killed her. The man Marina knew—the shelf-stocker who lived with his mother, a man's man, a smoker and a drinker, her coworker—seemingly posed no threat. She had known him, trusted him enough to introduce him to her son. In the case of Pichushkin, investigators suggested that he craved the attention of getting caught, purposefully choosing a victim that would lead to his arrest. What seems more likely based on his confession, is that when given the opportunity to kill Sasha simply couldn't resist.

Within hours of being apprehended, Pichushkin confessed to not only Marina's murder and the twelve others the police are aware of, but claimed he had killed as many as 63 people. Plying him with sandwiches and cigarettes, detectives finally begin to understand the scope of the disappearances and consequent murders in and around the ignored *khrushchevki*. Following standard procedure for murder cases, Pichushkin is taken to the scene of the murders to reenact them on film, eventually to be used as evidence in his trial. Due to the extensiveness of his crimes, what is typically only a few hours of video continues on for nearly 40 hours filmed over the course of a month.

While Pichushkin's trial is much less of a spectacle than that of his idol, Chikatilo, it is still well publicized and attended by an aggravated crowd of his victims' families. Despite his fluctuating claims of 62 to 64 murders, the official charges brought to trial on September 13th are for 49 counts of murder and 3 attempted murders. Where police had ignored the voices of the lower class and their accounts of missing friends and families, the press steps in. With Sasha's quiet and undocumented past, journalists take statements from family members of victims, neighbors from Pichushkin's building, even random members of the community, stitching together a story for the Chessboard Killer, no matter how fabricated.

The most notable aspect of the trial was possibly the lack of controversy surrounding such a large and well-reported case. With very little deliberation, Pichushkin's psychological evaluation deemed him sane, stating that "his actions were purposeful and consistent... he was aware of what he was doing." After meeting for only three hours, the jury unanimously ruled Pichushkin guilty on all counts. Pichushkin's defense team filed an appeal within weeks but it was denied immediately. The first fifteen years of Pichushkin's life sentence were ordered to be spent in solitary confinement in a northern high security prison, where he remains today.

Despite the severity of his sentence, the prosecutors and the family of his victims are still divided in their opinions of his punishment. The chief prosecutor told the press immediately after the trial let out that he believed that "justice has been done... He received the punishment that he deserved." In contrast, Tamara Klimmova, whose husband fell victim to Pichushkin, demanded more.

"He should be handed over to the public for punishment rather than allowed to live in prison at our expense."

Now nearly nine years into his sentence, Pichushkin continues to serve out his punishment in solitary confinement. Sasha will be 44 years old when he integrates back into communal prison life, just another member of Russia's growing prison population of almost six hundred fifty thousand people, lost in the crowd of the criminal justice system.

THE HILLSIDE STRANGLERS

NAOMI ROBERTS

Cousins Kenneth Bianchi and Angelo Buono, Jr. are collectively known by their media epithet "The Hillside Strangler". These two men were responsible for the murders of at least nine females, ages 12 to 28, during the late 1970s in Los Angeles, California, and Bianchi killed two more in Washington. After their first three victims did not gain much attention because they were prostitutes, Bianchi and Buono decided to abduct and murder middle-class "nice" girls. Five victims were found on hillsides in the Glendale-Highland Park area during Thanksgiving weekend in 1977 and the resulting panic led to the coining of the moniker "Hillside Strangler".

Lead Los Angeles Police Department homicide investigator Detective Sergeant Bob Grogan, along with his partner Dudley Varney as well as Los Angeles Sheriff's Department's Detective Frank Salerno, believed that the murders were the work of more than one killer but figured the less the murderers knew about what police knew the better.

Bianchi later moved to Washington where he murdered two more women before being caught.

Both Bianchi and Buono were convicted of multiple counts of first-degree murder and sentenced to life. Buono dies of a heart attack on 21 September 2002 while serving his time in Calipatria State Prison in Calipatria, California. Bianchi continues to serve his sentence at Washington State Penitentiary in Walla Walla.

Early Lives

Kenneth Bianchi

Kenneth Alessio Bianchi was born on 22 May 1951 in Rochester, New York, to a 17-year-old alcoholic prostitute who gave him up for adoption two weeks after he was born. He was adopted by Nicholas Bianchi and Frances Sciolono and despite a stable upbringing, Bianchi became a pathological liar at a very early age. Further, as a result of petit mal seizures he suffered at the age of five, Bianchi often daydreamt as if he were in a trance.

Bianchi suffered from insomnia and frequently wet the bed as a child (one of the triad symptoms of serial killers). Frances took him to the doctor on multiple occasions for his urination problem and being examined by the doctor caused Bianchi much embarrassment and humiliation. He also had a bad temper and was diagnosed with passive-aggressive personality disorder which is characterized by an individual who may appear to be enthusiastic about and actively comply with others' desires and needs while simultaneously resisting them, thus resulting in increased anger and hostility. At the core of this disorder is that the sufferer resents responsibility and instead of openly expressing his or her feelings, demonstrates said resentment through actions such as procrastination, forgetfulness, and inefficiency. Despite having a rather high IQ of 116, Bianchi was a chronic underachiever in school. When Frances took him to a psychologist, it was determined that Bianchi was overly dependent upon his mother.

On 2 January 1957, Bianchi fell off of a jungle gym and landed on his face. His mother then sent him to a private Catholic elementary school where he excelled in creative writing. In July 1963, Bianchi pulled down a six-year-old girl's pants after "spontaneously decid[ing] that he liked doing so".

His adoptive father died in 1964, thus leaving an unemotional Bianchi having to attend public high school where he joined a motorcycle club and dated frequently. His adoptive mother was forced to work and she was known for keeping Bianchi home from school for extended periods of time.

While in high school, Bianchi set high standards for his many girlfriends such as complete fidelity and outwardly absolute devotion; however, these standard did not apply to him.

He graduated in 1971 from Gates-Chili High School in Rochester and, soon after, married his high school sweetheart, Brenda Beck; however, the couple divorced after only eight months. Rumor has it that Brenda left without a word.

Bianchi enrolled at Monroe Community College to study police science and psychology after deciding that he wanted to become a police officer; however, after only one term he dropped out and then was rejected for several positions both in Rochester and, later, Los Angeles. Consequently, Bianchi worked a series of menial odd jobs, eventually becoming a jewelry store security guard for which he was fired for stealing and giving his girlfriends the stolen jewelry. He would steal from other employers over the years.

He then left Rochester and moved to Los Angeles in late 1975 at the age of 26.

Angelo Buono, Jr.

Angelo Anthony Buono, Jr. was born on 5 October 1934, also in Rochester, New York, to first-generation Italian-American immigrants originally from San Buono, Italy. His parents divorced when he was young and a five-year-old Buono moved to Glendale, California, with his mother Jenny and his sister Cecilia, where his mother supported the family by doing piecework in a shoe factory. Raised Catholic, this had no effect on Buono's development as a decent human being.

Buono displayed a very high interest in sex from a young age and when he was a teenager claimed that he had raped and sodomized number of girls. Buono idealized serial rapist Caryl Chessman, also known as "The Red Light Bandit", calling Chessman his hero but added that Chessman should have murdered his victims. He developed a deep loathing of women and desire to injure and humiliate them, including his mother who he would verbally abuse; however, he was emotionally tied to her until her death in 1978.

Buono began stealing cars and was sent to the Paso Robles School for Boys.

In 1955, Buono married his high-school sweetheart, Geraldine Vinal, who was 17 years old at the time, who he had impregnated; however, less than a week later he left her. She would later give birth to a son, Michael Lee Buono, on 10 January 1956. Buono filed for divorce and refused to pay child support or let his son call him "Dad". He was back in jail for car theft when his first son was born.

Later, he impregnated Mary Castillo who gave birth to his second son, Angelo Anthony Buono III, at the end of 1956 and then married her in 1957. The couple would have four more children: Peter in 1957, Danny in 1958, Louis in 1960, and Grace in 1962. In 1964, Buono was believed to have sexually assaulted his two-year-old daughter Grace; however, there is insufficient literature to know fully the circumstances of the allegation. Buono's second marriage to Castillo also ended in divorce that same year after she purported that he had been physically, emotionally, and sexually abusive toward her. In a last-ditch effort to reconcile with him, Castillo was "rewarded" with his handcuffing her and threatening to kill her at gunpoint. Castillo would later recount a night during the first year they were together where Buono tied her spread-eagled to the bedposts and "raped her so violently she was afraid that he was going to kill her" and "her pain seemed to him his greatest pleasure" and, thus, he had no qualms of hurting her and didn't seem to care that the children witnessed the abuse. He avoided paying child support again.

Buono married a third time in 1965 to a 25-year-old single mother named Nannette Campino and the couple had two children of their own: Tony in 1967 and Sam in 1969. Despite being treated as poorly as Mary Castillo had been, Campino feared for her life on a daily basis but stayed until he began to sexually abuse her 14-year-old daughter. Buono allegedly bragged that he raped his stepdaughter because "[s]he needs breaking in" and then turned her over to his sons for their pleasure. Campino finally took her children, filed for divorce, and fled the state in 1971.

Buono, again, was arrested for auto theft and was sentenced to one year in prison; however, due to his large family his sentence was suspended so he could work to support them.

Buono married yet again, on a whim, to a woman named Deborah Taylor; however, the couple did not live together, nor did they ever divorce.

In 1975, he became a car upholsterer and purchased his own place at 703 E. Colorado Street to live and work. Despite his abuse, cockiness, overbearing nature, and lack of good looks, Buono was considered very attractive by women, particularly younger ones who were usually naïve about sex so it was easy to convince them that his outrageous demands and proclivities were normal. Thus, he frequently forced women to engage in sex acts with him and began a relationship with a teenage girl whom he twice impregnated.

He was ugly inside and out; very coarse, vulgar, ignorant, selfish, and sadistic.

Bianchi and Buono Together

At the age of 41, Buono came into contact with his cousin Kenneth Bianchi, the latter who, in 1975, moved to California and in with his cousin. Bianchi found his older cousin with "dyed black hair, gold chains around his neck, a large gaudy turquoise ring on his finger, red silk underwear and a virtual harem of jailbait girls". Buono taught Bianchi how to use fake police badges in order to coerce free sex from prostitutes. When they needed money the two also became pimps for a short time until the two girls who worked for them—Sabra Hannan and Becky Spears—escaped after enduring relentless abuse by Buono. Bianchi, still desiring to become a police officer, applied for jobs at the Los Angeles Sheriff's and Glendale Police Departments but neither were hiring. He then procured employment with a title company and used his first paycheck on an apartment and a Cadillac, moving in with coworker Kelli Boyd. Boyd rejected his marriage proposal as she considered Bianchi to be very jealous, immature, and a liar; however, in May 1977 she told him she was expecting their first child together. The couple moved to an apartment at 1950 Tamarind Avenue in Hollywood.

Bianchi also rented some office space and set himself up as a psychologist with a fake degree and credentials. He did not have many clients and when Boyd found out she was outraged. During the "Hillside Strangler" investigation, Bianchi told Boyd he had lung cancer and was undergoing chemotherapy and radiation to explain for his work absences; however, this was a lie. One day, detectives came to his apartment to ask questions but were "favorably impressed" and did not consider him a suspect at that time.

The Murders

In October 1977, the two men committed their first murder together. Their M.O. was to cruise around Los Angeles and use fake badges to convince women that they were undercover police officers. After persuading them into Buono's car that the men said was an unmarked police car, the two would take their victims to Buono's house where they would rape, torture, and strangle them with their "signature" weapon—a garrote (a handheld ligature such as a chain, rope, or strap)—although some of their victims were reportedly killed by lethal injection, electric shock, and gas asphyxiation. Their bodies were thus disposed of outside, frequently in hilly areas.

Yolanda Washington, 19

19-year-old tall, leggy, African-American prostitute Yolanda Washington disappeared on 17 October 1977 from Cathedral City, California. She was found the next day dumped just outside Forest Lawn Cemetery, beaten, raped, and strangled with a piece of cloth. Her corpse was cleaned and there were faint marks around her wrists, ankles, and neck. Her body was posed in a grotesque sexual position.

Judith Lynn Miller, 15

On 31 October, 15-year-old Judith Lynn Miller, a runaway, was found in a La Crescenta-Montrose neighborhood, face up on a parkway in a residential area. The homeowner covered her with a tarp so that neighborhood children wouldn't see her. After the incident, that same homeowner relocated his family to another state.

The victim was small and thin, perhaps 90 pounds, with medium length reddish-brown hair. She had bruising around her neck. She had also been raped and sodomized and her body had been posed with her legs in a diamond-like position.

Los Angeles Sheriff's Department Sergeant Frank Salerno was called to the site. He noticed insect activity upon her skin and on her eyelid was "a small piece of light-colored fluff" that he saved for forensic experts. He surmised that she had been killed elsewhere and her body had been deliberately placed where it would quickly be found.

At her autopsy, the coroner determined that she had been killed around midnight and was raped and sodomized.

There was no missing person's report matching this latest victim so after a couple of days, Salerno had the newspapers run a small story on her with a request to contact the police if anyone could identify her. Still nothing. Salerno then took her picture to Hollywood Boulevard and showed it to hundreds of runaways, addicts, homeless people, and prostitutes. The name Judy Miller kept coming up as a young destitute prostitute. One man named Markust Camden—a self-proclaimed bounty hunter—told Salerno that he saw Judy Miller leave the local fish and chips restaurant at 9:00 p.m. the night before she was found dead. In fact, he would pick Buono out of a police photo lineup, but failed to recognize Bianchi.

Eventually, Salerno was able to track down the Miller family and got a positive identification. They had nothing useful to contribute to the investigation.

Elissa "Lissa" Teresa Kastin, 21

Lissa Kastin, 21, was working as a waitress at the Healthfaire Restaurant to pay for ballet lessons as she was an avid dancer. She also worked part time for her father's real estate and construction business. She was last seen leaving work the night of 5 November. She was found the next day near the Chevy Chase Country Club in Glendale on 6

November; which was also near to where Buono lived. She had been beaten, raped, and strangled to death.

Salerno compared notes with the Glendale Police Department and noticed similarities between his latest victim and this new one. Both bodies had the same five-point ligature marks—ankles, wrists, and neck—and had been dumped within six miles of each other. This latest victim had been raped but there was no evidence of sodomy.

When Salerno looked at the dump site he was confident that at least two men were involved due to the large guardrail between the street and where the body was found and the near impossibility that one man could have gotten her body over it alone.

Dolores Cepeda, 12 and Sonja Johnson, 14

After their early murders failed to attract much publicity, Bianchi and Buono decided to find some younger victims.

12-year-old Dolores Cepeda and 14-year-old Sonja Johnson were abducted in Highland Park, California, on 13 November. They had last been seen getting off a school bus heading home from St. Ignatius School and approaching a large two-tone sedan that, reportedly, had two men inside.

Both young girls were found on 20 November in the hills between Glendale and Eagle Rock, near Dodger Stadium by a young nine-year-old boy who was treasure hunting in the trash on the hillside.

Los Angeles Police Department Homicide Detective Dudley Varney had been called to this site.

Kristina Weckler, 20

That same day, 20-year-old Kristina Weckler was found on the other side of the same hillside where Cepeda and Johnson were found.

Weckler was a quiet, loving, and serious honors student at the Pasadena Art Center of Design and lived in Glendale.

She was found nude, raped, tortured, and strangled to death as evidenced by ligature marks on her neck, as well as around her wrists and ankles. She had blood oozing from her rectum and bruises on her breasts. Weckler was the first victim to show additional overt signs of torture; having been injected with Windex glass cleaner she had oozing injection marks on her arms.

Los Angeles Police Department Homicide Detective Sergeant Bob Grogan—Varney's partner—was called to this site. He noticed that there was no indication of any disturbance of the foliage in the area or evidence that the body had been dragged there. Grogan made a mental note that she likely had been killed elsewhere and then carried and dumped in this location by one or maybe two men.

At this point, police were entertaining the idea that there was more than one killer and that they were becoming increasingly more sadistic.

Jane Evelyn King, 28

28-year-old actress Jane King disappeared in Los Angeles around 10 November 1977, and was found near the Los Feliz off ramp of the Golden State Freeway on 23 November. She had been sodomized and strangled and her body was badly decomposed. After King was found, Los Angeles Police Department officials—in addition to Glendale Police Department and Los Angeles County Sheriff's Department officers—created a task force to catch the "Hillside Strangler".

Lauren Rae Wagner, 18

18-year-old student Lauren Wagner lived with her parents in the San Fernando Valley. Her parents had gone to bed on 28 November, expecting their daughter to return home before midnight. The next morning, they found her car parked across the street with the door ajar.

Wagner was found later that day in a wooded area near Glendale's Mount Washington area. She was lying partially in the street, nude, with ligature marks on her ankles, wrists, and neck. Wagner, too, had been tortured as the palms of her hands contained several burn marks.

At the dump site was also a "shiny track of some sticky liquid, which had attracted a convoy of ants". Police considered that if the substance was saliva or semen from the killer then, perhaps, his blood type could be determined, as tests on semen found inside the earlier victims revealed nothing. It was later found that Bianchi was not a secretor, in that his blood type could not be determined by other bodily fluids. DNA testing had not come into popularity at this time.

When Wagner's father questioned the neighbors, it turned out that the woman who lived in the house where his daughter's car was parked, Beulah Stofer, saw Wagner's abduction. Stofer said that Wagner had pulled over to the curb at around 9:00 p.m. and two men had parked their car beside hers. After some type of disagreement, Wagner "ended up in the car with the two men".

When Grogan went to talk to the neighbor, she told him that she had just had a phone call from a man with a New York accent who told her to "keep her mouth shut about what she had witnessed or he would kill her". Stofer also told Grogan that the car was a large dark sedan with a white top and that one of the men dragged Wagner from her car into his while Wagner protested, "You won't get away with this!" Stofer described one man as tall and young with acne scars while the other was older and shorter, Latin-looking, and with bushy hair. She said she was positive that she would identify them again. This statement rang true when she picked both Bianchi and Buono out of a photo lineup shown to her by Grogan.

Kimberly Diane Martin, 17

Tall, blonde prostitute Kimberly Martin, 17, disappeared from Echo Park, California, and was found strangled to death on 13 December 1977 on a steep hillside on Alvarado Street. Martin had worked for the Climax "modeling agency".

Police believed they had two reasonably good leads in this case. First, Martin's last "client" called her to 1950 Tamarind, apartment 114; however, this turned out to be a vacant apartment. Secondly, the murderer called from a payphone in the lobby of the Hollywood Public Library on Ivar Street. Unfortunately, nothing came from these leads.

Cindy Lee Hudspeth, 20

On 16 February 1978, 20-year-old Bible school teacher and secretary at an Echo Park church Cindy Hudspeth was found in the trunk of her bright orange 1977 Datsun B210 that had been pushed over a cliff on Angeles Crest in Los Angeles National Forest near La Canada. She had been raped and strangled, with the strangulation marks similar to those associated with the "Hillside Strangler".

Hudspeth was also a neighbor of Weckler even though the two women did not know each other. Interestingly, Bianchi also lived in the same apartment complex; however, this lead was never pursued even though both Grogan and Salerno believed that there was a good chance that at least one of the murderers lived in the Glendale area.

After this case, the lack of additional victims resulted in the disbanding of the "Hillside Strangler" Task Force.

Jill Barcomb, 18 (originally believed to be a Hillside Strangler victim)

18-year-old prostitute Jill Barcomb was abducted in Beverly Hills and found near the famous Hollywood sign on 9 November. Whereas it was originally believed that she was a victim of the "Hillside Strangler" because she had been raped, beaten, and strangled, in 2005, her death was conclusively proven through DNA analysis to have been committed by Rodney Alcala, the "Dating Game Killer".

Also, sometime in 1977, the two men gave Catharine Lorre a ride with the intent of killing her; however, when they learned that she was the daughter of famous actor Peter Lorre who played a child murderer in Fritz Lang's 1931 masterpiece film *M*, they let her go. She had no idea who the men were until they were arrested.

The two stopped killing after their ninth victim, Hudspeth (although at this time it was presumed they had ten victims with Barcomb), likely due to the birth of Bianchi's son and, as some surmise, that he had made some acquaintances within the Los Angeles Police Department who would take him on ride-alongs around the city, ironically, looking for the killers, and Bianchi could talk about nothing else while in police presence. On the night they had tried to abduct another victim, the two men got into a heated argument when Bianchi told his cousin that he had been questioned in the "Hillside Strangler" case. After Bianchi's confession about being questioned by police, Buono, furious, threatened to kill his cousin.

Bianchi's Washington Murders

Bianchi's girlfriend, Kelli Boyd gave birth to their son, Sean, in February 1978, and in March Boyd decided to return to her parents in Bellingham, Washington, as she was tired of both Los Angeles and Bianchi's lifestyle. After three months of pleading to be reunited, Boyd relented and Bianchi moved to Washington in May. Bianchi's role as boyfriend and father was relatively successful and he even took a job as a security guard, ultimately earning the trust of his supervisors. However, this way of life did little to alleviate Bianchi's murderous urges. Within six months he was actively looking for new victims.

On 11 January 1978, Bianchi lured two Western Washington University students—roommates Karen Mandic, 22, and Diane Wilder, 27—to a house he allegedly "guarded" under the pretense of housesitting. Once there, he raped, tortured, and murdered them.

On 12 January, police were informed that two female students were missing after Mandic's boss became worried that she didn't arrive at work that day. He did remember that she had told him she had accepted a housesitting job in a wealthy Bayside neighborhood from a security guard friend of hers. When former-priest-turned-Bellingham-Police-Chief Terry Mangan went to the girls' home he found a hungry cat, as well as the address of the home where they were to housesit. The name of one security guard kept coming up, as well as a record that Bianchi had used a company truck that same night, supposedly to take into the shop for repairs. This never happened. Mangan began to consider the fact that the women had met with foul play.

Police then went to the Bayside house and found a wet footprint. They also interviewed a neighbor who told them that a security guard asked her to check on the house except for the night the women disappeared because "there was special work being done to the alarm system and he didn't want her to be taken as an intruder".

After a press conference, a woman called police to report that a car had been abandoned near her home in a heavily-wooded area. In the car were the bodies of Mandic and Wilder. Both had bruising and had been strangled to death.

Mangan had the security guard picked up. He gave them no trouble. His name was Kenneth Bianchi.

There was ample forensic evidence in this case; most notably foreign pubic hairs on the girls and fibers from the house's carpet matching fibers on the dead girls' clothing and shoes. Additionally, when police searched Bianchi's home they found several items stolen from job sites where he worked.

Remembering back to the "Hillside Strangler" cases in Los Angeles—and knowing Bianchi had lived there—Mangan called the police departments in California who had worked on the task force. He spoke to Detective Frank Salerno to whom everything finally made sense. Detectives tirelessly worked to link Bianchi to the strangler cases and were confident that he was one of the murderers.

Investigation and Arrest

Bianchi was not as careful this time, having left significant clues, most notably his car with California license plates was seen and subsequently connected to the addresses of two Hillside Strangler victims. Without mastermind Buono, Bianchi didn't have the wherewithal to cover his tracks.

Bianchi was arrested the following day, on 12 January 1979.

Buono was arrested on 22 October 1979, after Bianchi told police about his cousin's complicity in the murders.

Trial and Conviction

Prior to his 1981 trial, Bianchi decided to plead not guilty by reason of insanity and claimed to have a separate personality named

"Steve Walker" who had committed the murders. After several interviews by experts specializing in multiple personality disorder and hypnosis, it was determined that he was faking. Immediately after Dr. Martin Orne mentioned to Bianchi that in genuine cases of multiple personality disorder there are typically at least three personalities, Bianchi created another alter ego named "Billy", shortly followed by two more. It was later determined that the name "Steven Walker" came from a student whose identity Bianchi had previously tried to steal to enable him to fraudulently practice psychology. Further, in Bianchi's apartment investigators found several psychology books which laid credence to Bianchi's ability to fake the disorder. He was eventually diagnosed with antisocial personality disorder with sexual sadism.

During trial, there was significant physical trace evidence against the two men; including fibers from Buono's upholstery from his home and workshop on two of the victims; an imprint of a fake police badge on his wallet; and hairs from rabbits he had raised on another victim.

Bianchi agreed to plead guilty and testify against his cousin in order to get leniency, albeit uncooperatively (evidence of his passive-aggressive personality disorder).

Judge Ronald M. George—who would later become California Supreme Court Chief Justice—said during Buono's sentencing hearing, "I would not have the slightest reluctance to impose the death penalty in this case were it within my power to do so. Ironically, although these two defendants utilized almost every form of legalized execution against their victims, the defendants have escaped any form of capital punishment." On an interesting side note, George's roommate at the time was author Darcy O'Brien who, four years after the trial, wrote a book about the case.

Both men were sentenced to life in prison.

While incarcerated, Buono married mother-of-three Christine Kizuka in 1986 while she was visiting her husband—and father of her children—who was in the cell next door to Buono at the Los Angeles

County Jail, serving 18 months for assault with a deadly weapon. She worked as a supervisor at the California State Employment Development Department.

Whereas the 64-year-old Bianchi continues to serve his life sentence at the Washington State Penitentiary in Walla Walla, Buono died of a heart attack on 21 September 2002 while serving life at Calipatria State Prison in Calipatria, California. Denied for parole on 18 August 2010, Bianchi will next be eligible for parole in 2025.

Aftermath

Bianchi is also a suspect in the "Alphabet Murders"—also known as the "Double Initial Murders"—which occurred in the early 1970s in his hometown of Rochester wherein three young girls were raped, strangled to death, and dumped in the wilderness. At the time he worked as an ice cream vendor situated near two of the murder sites. On 16 November 1971, ten-year-old Carmen Colon disappeared and was found two days later in Churchville, New York, 12 miles from where she was last seen. 11-year-old Wanda Walkowicz disappeared on 2 April 1973 and was found the next day in Webster, New York, off State Route 104, seven miles from Rochester. Finally, on 26 November 1973, Michelle Maenza, 11, disappeared and was found two days later in Macedon, New York, a mere 15 miles from Rochester. They were called the "Alphabet Murders" because not only did the young victims have the same initial for their first and last name but they were also found in cities which began with the same letter.

Whereas Bianchi has repeatedly tried to get his name cleared from these murders he remains a suspect because his vehicle was seen near two of the murder sites.

Another series of murders with similar circumstances occurred in California in the late 1970s and investigators have hypothesized that they are connected to the Rochester "Alphabet Murders". In 1977, Roxene Roggasch, Paula Parsons, and Carmen Colon (like one of the original "Alphabet Murder" victims) were found raped and dead.

Whereas Bianchi was tried for six murders, DNA exonerated him of the California "Alphabet Murders".

A 2008 movie entitled *The Alphabet Killer* was very loosely based upon the murders, and in 2010 a book written by Cheri Farnsworth called *Alphabet Killer: The True Story of the Double Initial Murders* was released.

In 1980, Bianchi started a relationship with a Veronica Lynn Compton, who was a defense witness during his trial. Compton, a cocaine addict who was fascinated by serial killers, was working as a scriptwriter in Hollywood. On one of her numerous visits with Bianchi while he was incarcerated, she gave him a copy of her screenplay entitled *The Mutilated Cutter*, about a female serial killer, and asked for this input. Compton grew increasingly fixated and allegedly fell in love with Bianchi. Later, she was convicted and incarcerated for attempting to strangle a cocktail waitress who she had lured to a hotel in a ploy to have the world—and authorities—believe that the real "Hillside Strangler" was still on the loose and that the wrong man was incarcerated. To make it look like an authentic "Hillside Strangler" murder, Bianchi manipulated and used Compton as a means to get out of prison by giving her semen of his smuggled out of the facility in a rubber glove to plant on the body. Despite that DNA forensics had not been utilized at that time, semen could still be analyzed to demonstrate the killer's blood type; however, Bianchi was not a secretor. The intended victim managed to get away and Compton was tried and convicted of first-degree attempted murder and sentenced to life. Compton was paroled from prison in 2003.

In 1992, Bianchi sued Catherine Yronwode for $8.5 million for putting an image of his face on a trading card. He claimed his face was his trademark. The case was dismissed with the judge saying that if Bianchi's face was, indeed, his trademark during the murders then he would not have tried to hide it from police.

In 2007, Buono's grandson, Christopher Buono, shot his grandmother—Mary Castillo who was married to Buono at one time—and then committed suicide. Christopher was unaware of his grandfather's true identity until 2005.

Bianchi and Buono are immortalized in film. The 1989 film *The Case of the Hillside Stranglers*—based on O'Brien's book—starred Dennis Farina as Buono and Billy Zane as Bianchi. In the 2004 film *The Hillside Strangler*, Buono was portrayed by actor Nicholas Turturro and Bianchi was portrayed by C. Thomas Howell.

The 2006 movie *Rampage: The Hillside Strangler Murders* starred Tomas Arana as Buono and Clifton Collins, Jr. as Bianchi.

In 2001 the Discovery Channel aired an episode of *The New Detectives* that revisited the murders.

Bianchi and Buono have also been mentioned several times on the television show *Criminal Minds* as an example of killer teams with psychopathic predatory sexual sadist personalities who murdered their victims together.

THE SUFFOLK STRANGLER

JASMINE GREY

Steven Gerald James Wright was considered to be an ordinary, everyday English barman. Friends and family thought that his gambling addiction and his relationship issues were the brunt of his problems, but little did they know that was only scratching the surface of his nasty habits. He followed into the footsteps of the British serial killers that had come before him, like the legendary "Jack the Ripper", by primarily preying on the prostitutes of the red light district. Steven Wright is better known as "The Suffolk Strangler" or "The Ipswich Ripper" and he is currently serving a life imprisonment for the murders of five young women: Tania Nicol, 19-years-old; Gemma Rose Adams, 25-years-old; Anneli Sarah Alderton, 24-years-old; Annette Nicholls, 29-years-old; Paula Lucille Clennell, 24-years-old. All of these innocent women were murdered while working the corners of the red light district in Suffolk. The two-month-long murder spree received mass media attention and pushed the entire Suffolk area into utter panic. The heinous nature of the Suffolk Strangler's crimes, the mystery of his identity, the body count, and the mass hysteria pushed the police department into a full-scale investigation. After hard work, persistence, DNA evidence, and a few false leads, the police finally linked Steven Wright to the Ipswich Ripper.

Early Life

Steven Gerald James Wright was born on April 24, 1958, in Erpingham[1], a Norfolk village in the United Kingdom. His father Conrad was a military policeman and his mother Patricia was a veterinary nurse. As the second eldest of four children, with one older brother and two younger sisters, Wright claimed to live in an unhappy household. Patricia Wright divorced Conrad on the claims of domestic violence and abandoned the family when Steven was only 9-years-old.

After he was arrested for the murders of five women, Steven sent a letter to his father that suggested a childhood full of violence and anger that could explain his violent nature: "Dear Dad, this is a reply to your letter you are right you have never seen me angry before because I am a quite [quiet] and placid person whenever I get upset I tend to bury it deep inside which I suppose is not a healthy thing to do because the more I do that the more withdrawn I become because I have seen to [too] much anger and violence in my childhood to last anyone a lifetime. But what really makes me sad is the fact that I thought all the family feuds were behind me now I really thought we had made a step forward I just wish everyone would get along and work towards a family unit because all the bickering and point scoring against each other is really getting me down it seems you are pulling me one way and Pam is pulling me the other and in the end, something will give and it just seems to me that person will be me and that is the last thing that I want at the moment has I am sure you do as well because if I start to fall apart at the seams I don't think I could cope in here I need to be strong to cope with this nightmare like that but you said in the paper that when you looked into my eyes you would know whether I was guilty or not that really hurt me it was like a knife in the heart for you to even contemplate that I could even be capable of such a terrible crime."

Conrad Wright, his father, claims that he does not know what his son is talking about. He denies the abuse that Steven refers to and

---

1.　　https://en.wikipedia.org/wiki/Erpingham

insists that he had a partially normal childhood. He was known to bottle up his anger and hyperventilate until he passed out. "He must be a raving lunatic," Conrad admitted after attending every trial in his son's defense. Conrad recalls his son during childhood as being quiet and introspective. Steven was also known to love horror films, Conrad explained later, "I was watching a film about a stranger and I thought how Steve loved horror films. He'd be jumping up and down, really into it."

Soon after he left school in 1974, Wright joined the Merchant Navy and became a chef on the ferries that sailed from Felixstowe, Suffolk. He developed a name for himself as a "ladies man" because he was always seen with women and rarely without a girlfriend. When Wright was only 20-years-old he met his first wife and the mother of his first child, Angela O'Donovan. They married soon after they met, in 1978, but the couple separated just ten years later, in 1987. This would start a pattern of failed relationships that would slowly chip away at Wright's mental stability. Wright would later make three suicide attempts after splitting with his wife and/or girlfriend.

After the divorce, Wright worked many odd jobs, including at QE2, where he soon used prostitutes to heal the pain from his recent split. Wright claims that this was when his indulgence with sex workers truly began; he would begin visiting specific parlors and ports whenever he "got the urge". He was working in the onboard shop on QE2 when he met a young stewardess named Diane Cassell. In August of 1987, Wright married Diane Cassell at Braintree register office. Not unlike his first marriage, his marriage to Diane did not turn out to be a happy one. Wright and Cassell's marriage was full of abuse and neglect. Elizabeth Roche, a former next-door neighbor, explains that abuse nature that Steven Wright did not attempt to hide from friends and family, "Steve used to strangle Diane right in front of us. He would pin her up against the wall and put both hands around her throat. There were, at least, three times when he did it in front of witnesses. It would end when either my ex-husband or I would pull him off or he would come to his senses." Steven Wright seemed to often portray sudden, violent mood swings and fits of aggression, Roche went on to explain her former neighbor, "He had an ability to have a violent row one minute and then have a calm conversation with you straight afterward as if nothing had happened. The only way I can describe it is to say he was a real Jekyll and Hyde character. He definitely had a psycho side to him." Due to their dysfunctional and violent relationship, Wright separated from his second wife nearly a year after their wedding date – they divorced in 1988. "The marriage was a nightmare," Diane Cassell later stated, "It was an awful time which I would rather forget. I was glad when it ended. It didn't even last a year and he went off with someone else."

In 1989, Wright was working at the White Horse pub in Chislehurst when he began his four-year-long relationship with Sarah Whiteley. They moved to Plumstead where they had a daughter in 1992. Sarah described Steven Wright as a kind, generous, loving father. While in Plumstead Wright managed the Rose and Crown Pub. Wright had finally managed to be in a stable environment for the first time in his life, but it didn't last very long. This all came crashing down when the weight of Wright's addictions became too much for him to control. Steven lost his job and his newly found family due to his heavy drinking and frivolous gambling. After he lost the pub, Steve moved back to Felixstowe, where he worked odd jobs, but never accumulated much wealth because of his spending habits. Most of his hard earned money went to prostitutes and sex workers.

It was pretty well known that Wright's mental condition was not very stable after his second split up. Wright drowned his emotional and financial issues with gambling, drinking, and engaging with prostitutes, which only increased the mountain of debt that was hanging over his head. Steven Wright tried to commit suicide for the first time in 1994, when he locked himself in his garage, in a running vehicle, in hopes of carbon monoxide poisoning. This attempt was a failure and he was pulled out of the car by police before it was too late. His family and loved ones were in shock. Steven's half-brother Keith Wright explained the reasoning behind his brother's brash actions, "He just got himself into so much debt. I suppose he couldn't find a way out." Wright's financial issues were increasing at a dramatic level, falling apart as he tried to fund his addictions. In an attempt to earn money, Steven Wright bought a £13,000 car on hire purchase then sold it. Simultaneously Wright continued to charge his credit card, creating huge bills and adding to the debt that would eventually get him arrested for stealing £80 from the cash register at work. Nearly £40,000 worth of debt was racked up before he fled to Thailand and declared himself bankrupt.

The most interesting part of Wright's life was the very short time that he spent in Thailand to run away from the debt he accumulated in England. In Thailand, Steven spent most of his time spending money on Thai prostitutes. Somchit Chomphusaeng was a Thai woman who claimed to marry him while he was hiding away in 1999. After their two week honeymoon, Wright flew back to Britain and never returned to see his wife again. She received a letter shortly after his departure from a woman who claimed to be his mother. The letter told Somchit Chomphusaeng that Wright had been murdered, or in more gruesome details, had been stabbed to death. She saw her husband again years after his untimely "death" when photographs of Wright were released from his arrest in Ipswich. Upon first seeing the photograph, his "widow" claimed that she fainted from pure shock. Later, when she was in the proper mindset, she explained her husband's deception: "It must be his ghost. I was told he'd been murdered."

A Life shared in Ipswich

Steven Wright met Pamela Wright in 2001 in Felixstowe, Suffolk. Their shared last name have no hereditary connection, but they immediately hit it off and Pamela stayed by his side throughout the guilty verdict of the murder trial. In 2004, Steven and Pamela moved into a rented apartment in the center of Ipswich, Suffolk, which was very popularly known as the red light district where sex workers sold their trade for anyone who had the money. Steven worked as a forklift driver on the docks of Suffolk as Pamela worked at a call center. Soon after the move, Pamela took up the night shift at her job, which gave her partner plenty of free time to indulge in his habits. The increased and late night hours made Steven and Pamela's sex life virtually nonexistent. His girlfriend was completely unaware that the change in their sex life, and the increased about of time that Steven would be alone, would result in the deaths of five innocent women. Wright now had the freedom visit local prostitutes any time that he "got the urge" and he took advantage of the situation. After Steven dropped his unsuspecting girlfriend off at work, he spent the late night hours prowling streets of the Ipswich red light district, which was where he captured and preyed on his victims.

Steven created quite a name for himself in Ipswich, as he frequently visited the girls in the red light district. He was nicknamed by the sex workers as the "Mondeo Man" because of the car that he drove, the "Silver-backed gorilla" because of his hair color, and the "Soldier" because he wore camouflage pants from time to time. Most of the women didn't feel comfortable engaging with him because of his out of the ordinary behavior. He was very unlike most of their clientele because he seemed too angry and he seemed to ask too many questions, claimed a former sex worker in a later documentary interview. Some of the sex workers went into vivid descriptions on how he would cruise the red light district dressed in high heels, a PVC skirt, and a wig, masquerading as a woman as he tried to pick up prostitutes. One

Norwich worker explained from personal experience, "If you didn't get in the car he would get naked and just sit there with the headlights on. He freaked me out. The police knew about him." Her statement was proven right when Detective Chief Superintendent of the Ipswich murder investigation Stewart Gull stated that Wright was a pretty well-known curb crawler around this point in his life.

The Murders and the Investigation

Between the dates of October 30th and December 12th of 2006, Steven Wright murdered five sex workers from the Ipswich area. This string of murders took Suffolk by storm and sex workers everywhere were terrified that the Suffolk Strangler would pick them up next. These girls had few similarities despite their location, their occupation, and the drug habits that forced them to put themselves in an extremely vulnerable set of circumstances. All of these women were down on their luck and none of them were over the age of thirty when they made the fatal mistake of getting into the black Mondeo that belonged to Suffolk Strangler.

Tania Nicol was only 19-years-old when she encountered the Suffolk Strangler. On the freezing cold night of October 30th, 2006, the young girl left her home at eleven o'clock to service the curb crawlers of Ipswich's red light district. Sometime during that night, Tania willing stepped into Steven Wright's vehicle without hesitation, which hinted that Tania already knew him and did not expect anything unusual out of the situation, but when they pulled away from the curb the 19-year-old girl was never to be seen alive again. Usually, when Tania had a client she always made a point to keep her friends and colleagues updated on her whereabouts at all times. This night, however, Tania's friends did not receive the usual update. Tania didn't come home that night or any night after that. Tania's mother, who was unaware of her daughter's lifestyle at the time, reported the disappearance to the police 48 hours after she'd gone missing. The Suffolk police department regarded Tania as a high-risk target because of her profession and immediately took steps to discover her whereabouts. Detective Chief Superintendent Stewart Gull explained her disappearance in a documentary interview later, "She had literally disappeared off the face of the earth. Her phone record showed us a very flat line from the 1st of November. No incoming or outgoing movement of data at all..." The Suffolk police had absolutely no leads to point them towards the missing girl, so they took to the public to find anyone who knew the whereabouts of Tania Nicol. Little did they know that while they were investigating the disappearance of one woman, another was in danger of falling into the same trap that caught Tania.

The name of the second victim was Gemma Rose Adams. Gemma was last seen on the night of November 14th when she boarded a train after visiting with her mother. She was only 25-years old. Much like Tania, Gemma always kept people updated on her location through texts and calls, but on that cold November night, the calls stopped coming. Her boyfriend, worried because Gemma wasn't answering his text messages, reported her disappearance on November 15th. The similarities between Gemma and Tania's profession, location, and disappearance, drew police to the conclusion that these cases were linked, and were most likely done by the same man, or same group of men. Upon this realization, the Suffolk police immediately stepped up their efforts to find the young girls and began to question random, passing motorists in the red light district for information on the girls' whereabouts. One of these random, passing motorists was actually Steve Wright. When he was stopped and questioned on his relationship with Tania Nicol and Gemma Adams, he claimed that he didn't know them. "We distributed some 20,000 leaflets around the area," Andy Henwood, an investigator, explained in an interview, "...we set up road checks at periodic times after the disappearances. We interviewed some 400 people in respect to Tania's disappearance and some 300 people in respect to Gemma's disappearance." Despite the efforts of the Suffolk police, they never received any leads to the whereabouts of these two missing women. As the weeks passed by, the investigators who had been hopeful to find the two girls were beginning to give up the notion that they were alive.

On the morning of the December 2nd, Gemma's body was found in a Hintlesham river by water bailiff, Trevor Saunders. "I noticed what

I'd thought, at first, was a dummy, a mannequin. So I got down into the water to get it out," Saunders described his encounter with the body that he found upon checking the creek, "So I got down to pick it out, to clear the blockage, and when I got down to her, that when I realized that it [weren't] a dummy. It was a real body and I immediately thought to myself that I had found one of the missing girls." Due to the deposition of her body, Gemma's cause of death could not be established. She was naked when they discovered her, but there were no signs of sexual assault.

After Gemma's body was found, the police began a full-scale investigation to find the body of the assumed dead Tania Nicol. Despite the freezing cold temperatures, a team of divers swept through the disposition spot to find at least one strand of evidence. Less than a week later, Tania Nicol's naked body was discovered in a brook near Copdock Mill, less than two miles away from where Gemma's body was discovered. "Not in my wildest dreams did I anticipate that they would uncover the body of Tania Nicol," DCS Stewart Gull recalled, "We were no longer dealing with two missing persons. This was now a double murder inquiry."

A post mortem took place on both of the victims, but there were no concrete causes of death, due to the terrible shape of the bodies when they were discovered. It was obvious that the women died from lack of oxygen, but no tests could be made to find the culprit of the heinous crime. Ray Palmer, forensic scientist, explained the difficulty he had with retrieving evidence from the bodies, "...because it had been present in flowing water for a number of weeks, any prospect of recovering fibers or other debris for the skin, or any DNA from the skin, in that period of time was virtually zero."

The Suffolk Police department, which investigated an average of six murders per year, was not prepared for the two murders that took place in a matter of six days. The way that the bodies were disposed caused extra issues for investigators, "The bodies of Gemma Adams and Tania

Nicol were found in fast flowing, very cold water, and the problem that presented from our perspective was because of the emersion of water, any trace evidence that was present was most likely to be destroyed or washed away." The Ipswich Ripper's choice of deposition location made investigators extremely wary about who they were dealing with, as they realized that they were dealing with a cold and calculating murderer. "The fact that he had placed the bodies in water so as to destroy any forensic evidence, suggested to me that this was a very, what criminologists would describe as an 'organized' killer. By 'organized' I mean that he carefully thought through how he's crucially going to avoid being detected by the police," explained criminologist, Prof. David Wilson.

Anneli Sarah Alderton was 24-years-old when she was last seen on the night of December 3rd. Her body was discovered just days after the first two victims, in a woodland near Amberfield School on December 10th. Alderton was the very first body to show up on dry land. She was found naked and sexually assaulted, but the most disturbing part of the scene was that her corpse was posed in a cruciform position. Unlike the other victims, Anneli Alderton's body had not been deposited in water, so it might've had traces of evidence that could actually lead investigators to the murderer. Forensic scientists immediately combed the scene for any shred of DNA they could find. Investigator Gull explained how he felt after the discovery of Alderton's body in an interview, "Once Anneli Alderton's body had been found, we were clearly into a different realm. It looked very much like we had a serial killer on our hands. It clearly had very obviously linked murder investigations in a very close area around Ipswich and all the indications of that stated that it was the work of one man, or men working together."

The discovery of three murder victims in less than a week lead criminologist, David Wilson, to the conclusion that they were dealing with a serial killer, "When the third body turned up I think I was the

first person to say there is a serial killer on the loose in Ipswich and I think those words, I chose with a great deal of care because they were, as far as I was concerned, accurate and they also should've suggested, which I think they did, the gravity of the circumstances." Reporters all over the world flocked to Ipswich upon the news of three bodies. "What happened overnight as this crisis was developing was that the streets became filled with only one group of people and that group of people was journalists. Journalists seemed to be bumping into each other desperately hoping to find a prostitute that they could interview.
"

Despite the fact that there was a serial killer in the area, targeting only prostitutes, business did not slow in Ipswich's red light district. Ipswich was a prominent area for drugs and the majority of prostitutes worked the streets so they could fund their drug addictions. This provided an ideal situation for the Suffolk Strangler. The police put out a clear message that warned all sex workers against putting themselves in a life threatening situation, but not many listened. All the working girls that were interviewed admitted that they were scared, but that did not stop them from working. These women had addictions to feed and bills to pay, and sadly, even a murderer wasn't enough to keep them away from the curb crawlers of the red light district.

"Is it my turn, tonight? Am I not going to come home tonight? But what choice have I got but to go out there?" Sarah, a woman who worked the streets of Ipswich, explains the terror that she experienced during this time, "Cars would come by and you'd be praying that they would pick you up to get money, but you're praying that they wouldn't because you don't want them to do what they're going to do." Paula Clennell, the Ipswich Ripper's final victim, was interviewed by an Anglia News reporter only a month before her body was discovered. Paula agreed that she was afraid of the disappearances, but she admitted that it was not enough to keep her away from the money that she desperately needed. "I need the money," She shrugged with her back turned to the camera. Paula Clennell died less than two months later, at the hands of the Suffolk Strangler.

Annette Nicholls was 29-years-old when her body was found on December 12. Nicholls was naked when she was discovered by investigators in the same woods that Anneli Alderton was found. Her corpse was posed in a cruciform position, just like Gemma Adams. Police searched the woodland overhead when an observer from the helicopter inspecting team, Maggie Williams, made another shocking discovery: the body of a 24-year-old Paula Lucille Clennell. A post mortem confirmed that Paula Clennell died from compression to the neck, but the cause of Annette's death could not be established.

After finding five murdered women in the matter of six weeks, DCS Stewart Gull reluctantly announced to the public that they were dealing with a full-fledged serial killer, "Although we only had the cause of death for two [women], in all probability they all died as a result of some form of interference with the airway. So you put all of that together and I think quite rightly, we drew the conclusion that we were looking for just one or more persons, who were involved together in the abduction and murder of all five women." Gull stated. The 600 officers and staff of the Suffolk police department were joined by 500 members from all over the country. It was the biggest manhunt that had ever been conducted in eastern England.

Media presence increased in this area tenfold, which eventually drew the attention of a very odd character named Tom Stephens. The 37-year-old man admitted in an interview with a newspaper that he personally knew all of the victims. It wasn't long after the interview when Tom was taken into custody. "The police had to arrest Tom Stephens on that occasion because he said, 'I knew all of these five women, they've all been back to my house, I do not have an alibi for the nights that they went missing,'" Explained Professor David Wilson, "In those circumstances the police would've been bonkers not to arrest somebody who is openly saying that."

Tiny amounts of DNA were retrieved from the bodies of Anneli Alderton, Annette Nicholls, and Paula Clennell. The DNA all link back to the same person Steve Wright. Wright used gloves in an attempt to keep all his crime scenes clean from his DNA, but he didn't consider the DNA sample that he left in Birmingham from his previous offenses. This sample sat in a national database until it matched the fibers that were found on the victims. Eventually, this forensic evidence released Tom Stephen's from custody and shined a light on the true Suffolk Strangler.

The Trial

After Wright was identified he was put under 24-hour investigation where the police followed his every move. Early in the morning on December 19th, the police arrested Steve Wright from his Ipswich home. When he was questioned by the police Wright refused to speak. Any questions would be answered with the phrase "no comment". During the first eight outs of interrogation, he recited that line over and over again. Even without a confession, the forensic evidence was enough to charge Steven Wright for the murders of all five women on December 21st, 2006.

Wright's trial began on January 16, 2008, at the Ipswich Crown Court. The only case in Wright's defense was the argument that Wright was a frequenter of prostitutes in this area, although he denied using prostitutes during the interrogation, which would explain why his DNA was found on three of the young girls' bodies. He focused on Tania Nichols, telling a story about how he picked her up with the intention to have sexual relations, but changed his mind and returned her back to the red light district. Again, this account differed from the one that he originally gave to investigators. On February 21, 2008, Steve Wright was charged as guilty on all five counts of murder after eight hours of deliberation. He received a life sentence without any chance of parole. On February 22, 2008, Wright was taken to prison, where he'll be forced to live out the rest of his years behind bars.

Wright is still alive to this day and he is having a terrible time in prison. His twisted state of mind after imprisonment is outlined in his letter to his father: "...I just wish everyone would get along and work towards a family unit because all the bickering and point scoring against each other is really getting me down it seems you are pulling me one way and pam is pulling me the other and in the end, something will give and it just seems to me that person will be me and that is the last thing that I want at the moment has I am sure you do as well because if I start to fall apart at the seams I don't think I could cope in here I need to be strong to cope with this nightmare like that but you said in the paper that when you looked [in] my eyes you would know whether I was guilty or not that really hurt me it was like a knife in the heart for you to even contemplate that I could even be capable of such a terrible crime. You say you want to help me the only way that will happen is if you make the effort to work together because all this he said she said you must understand is not doing my frame of mind any good I just want it to stop I do love you dad..."

Conclusion

The Suffolk Strangler still impacts the lives of people today and his memory lives on to serve as a gruesome reminder that there are always predator's lurking in the shadows. The evilest thing in the world doesn't appear intimidating or off-putting; it appears normal and safe so that it can take advantage of a situation when it is too late to run. The memories of the five innocent women that were brutally murdered by this cold blooded killer, Tania Nicol, Gemma Rose Adams, Anneli Sarah Alderton; Annette Nicholls, and Paula Lucille Clennell, will live on far beyond the young girls' untimely deaths. Hopefully, the victim's family found comfort knowing that the Ipswich Ripper is no longer prowling the streets, waiting to find his new victim. Criminologist Professor David Wilson explained, "What's intriguing about serial killers is not the fact that they are the epitome of evil, but rather they are the banality of evil. It is their ordinariness that sticks out and when I first got to know more about the background of Steve Wright, what struck me was again, that sense of the everyday nature of who serial killers are." Steven Wright was a serial killer in all meanings of the world; cold, heartless, with a complete lack of conscience.

The Racist Serial Killer

Nancy Meghan White

In Kansas City, Missouri, on August 18, 2017, Fredrick Demond Scott, age 22, was arrested and charged with two counts of first-degree murder and two counts of armed criminal action in the shooting deaths of John Palmer, aged 54, and Steven Gibbons, aged 57— the first and the last victims of the Indian Creek Murders. The Indian Creek Murders consisted of five white, middle-aged men. All were shot from behind and all except the last were shot on the walking and biking trails known as The Indian Creek Trail, thus the name Indian Creek Murders. Although Scott was arrested and charged on August 18, 2017, Jackson County Prosecutor Jean Peters Baker did not officially announce his arrest until August 27, 2017, when it was also announced that Scott was the suspect in the other three murders along the Indian Creek Trail.

These five murders happened over a span of nine months from August 2016 until April 2017 in a killing spree that left Kansas City men afraid to walk along trails alone and took police a year to solve only two of them.

After his arrest, Scott told investigators first that the gun fired accidentally as he pulled it from his pocket. Then police gathered DNA evidence that linked Scott to both the Gibbons and the Palmer murder scene. Scott then admitted to killing both men. Later, in an interview with investigators, Scott mumbled, "they [the victims] never saw it coming."

Scott told police that he was upset over the 2015 shooting death of his half brother, Gerrod Woods, with whom he had a very close relationship.

Gerrod was Scott's half brother by their father Tyrone Scott. However, his mother La'Kesha and her husband, Gerald Woods, Sr who adopted Gerrod, giving him the Woods last name, raised Gerrod.

Fredrick Scott was raised by his mother and has four living siblings, all of whom wish to remain anonymous. Scott's mother has said that Scott began exhibiting symptoms of paranoid schizophrenia at about the age of 16, as did his older brother. Scott, however, refused to get treatment for his condition and it worsened over the years.

On April 7, 2013, Scott's mother called police on him during an argument and in 2014, Scott was in court for assaulting his mother. Scott's mother says she was trying to get him to seek professional help at a mental health clinic for the paranoid schizophrenia. Scott was an adult and she could not force him to go. She did tell him on two occasions that he would have to move out if he did not "get himself together and get help." An argument erupted and Scott shoved her several times. This assault resulted in her calling the police. In January of 2014, while attending his senior year at Center Alternative School in Kansas City, Missouri, Scott found himself in trouble for saying that he wanted to "shoot the school up Columbine-style" and "kill the white people." Scott's mother said he never had any hatred toward white people that she knew about and that he even did odd jobs for a few white men. He received a suspended 180-day sentence for the threat against the Center Alternative School. Public records show that Scott was picked up for shoplifting in 2016.

Despite his troubles, Scott finished his term at Center Alternative School and graduated and received his diploma at the age of 20 after repeating his senior year. "His teachers and his principal were very supportive of him," Scott's mother said. "They really worked with him over there."

Scott worked odd jobs and had a job at a local Burger King in the vicinity of the murders. It is still unclear whether the killings were racially motivated, and some people are asking if one racist statement in the past can make these killings "hate crimes" or not.

People who know Scott said his half brother's murder sent him over the edge.

"He felt like his brother was the only person in the world who loved him," one of his Burger King co-workers told the Star. "It really damaged him."

In December of 2015, Scott's half brother Gerrod Hassan Woods, aged 23, was shot and killed along with another man during a robbery. This is the incident he cited as having him upset when he was arrested for the Gibbons murder. However, a black man killed his half brother, while Scott's victims were white, middle-aged men, most of them walking alone with their dogs. Gibbons was the exception. Video surveillance shows Scott follow Gibbons off a city bus. He then shot Gibbons and proceeded to turn around and get back on another bus. Therefore, Gibbons was shot on a city street whereas the other men were shot on the Indian Creek Trail or very near it.

Later, it was discovered that Scott had reported handguns as being stolen on four separate occasions. When asked if four separate stolen gun reports would not raise some red flags, Kansas City Police Captain, Stacey Graves said the department could not discuss the case against Fredrick Scott because the investigation is ongoing and still open, but she agrees that the stolen gun reports should have "raised some red flags." According to court documents that outline all five killings, the first three happened within days, and even hours, of Scott's stolen gun reports. Concerning the stolen gun reports, Graves also said, "That is something that is being investigated. It will be something we look at." It is still unclear when the fourth gun was reported stolen.

Of all the guns used in the killings, police have recovered only the 9 mm handgun, which, according to court records, Scott told detectives he used to kill Gibbons.

Scott had reported that gun stolen, also. Even though he denied any involvement in three of the killings, Scott told investigators he reported the guns stolen to disassociate himself from the killings.

Mark Jones of Chicago, a retired supervisory special agent in the ATF, said police should follow up immediately when someone reports a second gun theft because the victim is either complicit in the theft or the victim needs to better secure and protect firearms from theft. "I can see where you can report a gun stolen because you know it is going to be used in a crime, but I think you can only get away with that once," Jones said.

Kansas City Police Chief, Rick Smith, said at least 50 law enforcement personnel have worked on the investigation of the killings. The FBI assisted. On Tuesday, Smith said he extended his condolences to the families of the victims.

Police suspect that Fredrick Scott used the guns he reported stolen to commit these crimes and then reported them stolen to throw off investigators.

Brian Darby told The Star that he feels disrespected by the account given by Scott's mother that he suffers from paranoid schizophrenia. He feels the schizophrenia will be used as a defense for Scott.

THE INDIAN CREEK MURDERS:

Five middle-aged white men fatally shot from behind in sneak attack murders in Kansas City, Missouri. All victims were between ages 54 and 67, male, white, all but one were walking their dogs along Indian Creek Trail and in at least two cases, the dogs stayed by their slain owners until police arrived. The profiles of the victims made them relatively rare among Kansas City homicide victims. Some of the men were killed while walking their dogs.

The unsolved killings mystified Kansas City residents and spread fears of a serial killer.

First victim: John Palmer, aged 54, was shot several times, including in the back and his body dragged off the trail into the woods. He was found August 19, 2016 off East Bannister Road and Lydia Avenue in the small wooded area near the Indian Creek Trail. Police found a t-shirt at the scene with DNA that matched Fredrick Scott—who, a year later, under arrest for the Gibbons killing, admitted killing Palmer. Palmer was a man, who relatives said, liked to go on long walks through nature. Palmer's first cousin, Janelle Kristian of Olathe county, said he was, "a man of integrity, honesty and caring."

They grew up in the same household as children according to KANSASCITY.COM.

Second victim: David Lenox, aged 67,was found dead of a gunshot to the back of his head, only a few feet from his front door where he was walking one of his dogs, in the 9900 block of Walnut Street on February 27, 2017. A single .380-caliber shell casing lay close by the body. The police report that Lenox's dog stayed by his body until they arrived.

Third victim: Timothy S. Rice of Excelsior Springs, aged 57, was found dead on April 4, 2017, inside a shelter at Minor Park near East Red Bridge Road and 110th Street. He had been shot multiple times, including in the head. Police found several 9mm shell casings at the scene. Two hours after Rice was found, Scott reported a 9mm handgun stolen.

Hannah Rice, daughter of third victim, Timothy Rice, opened up about her dad and said she wanted the public to know him. "My dad was one of the friendliest people you could ever meet, he didn't know a single stranger," Hannah Rice wrote about her father in an email to The Star Monday evening.

She said in her message that her dad, who had been an electrician most of his life, "could make conversation with anyone at anytime." And, she said that after 13 years of being divorced, her dad and mom had remained friends and had lunch together on the day he died.

"I will always remember how he loved taking me as a child on hikes and fishing trips, we always would compete on who could catch the most fish. My father wasn't perfect by any means but he had a genuine heart," Hannah Rice wrote.

"No one ever expects something like this to happen in your life. To have your loved one brutally taken away from you," she said, adding that her heart goes out to the other four families who also lost loved ones.

Her message thanked Kansas City police for all their hard work on the murders. "They have done a phenomenal job chasing leads and working nonstop to catch this violent person," she said.

Hannah Rice also called for the public to provide police with help in the case.

"I also want to urge anyone to come forth with any information you may have no matter how small," she wrote. "It may just be the right information KCPD needs to see all of our families the justice we deserve."

Fourth victim: Michael Darby, aged 61, was found dead on May 18, 2017 from a single gunshot to the back of the head, along Indian Creek Trail off 103rd Street, about a half-mile east of the popular Coach's Bar & Grill where he was a co-owner. The bar was closed by flooding a month ago and may never reopen. The police found a single .22-caliber shell casing near the crime scene. The victim's son, Brian Darby, wonders if more could have been done to prevent the last deaths, including that of his father.

In June 2017, police released a 29-second surveillance video showing a man walking along Indian Creek—a man who police thought might have vital information about the killing in May of Coach's co-owner, Michal Darby. The Kansas City police asked the public for information on June 27, 2017, stating that the person in the video was not considered a suspect in the homicide.

Scott, after his arrest, admitted that he was the man shown in the surveillance video circulated by the Kansas City police department.

Brian Darby says he feels disrespected by the claims of Scott's mother that her son was suffering from paranoid schizophrenia at the time of the murders.

Scott's mother, added that maybe in jail he'd finally get help: "I don't want those demons in him anymore because a person who has never dealt with paranoid schizophrenia — you don't know what it's like. It's hell. Their life is hell."

A lot of people would just as soon not hear that. First, citing a mental illness is seen as making an excuse, which is seen, by many as an affront to the victims and their loved ones.

After the loss of his father and then his father's business, it is quite easy to understand why he would question the motives of Scott's mother in speaking about her son's mental state. Or why he scoffs at the comment that she "says she's hurting just as much as the families of the victims. My father will never get his morning walk again. He'll never see the sun again. He won't get his three meals a day, which her son still has."

In the middle of a rather hot political argument over whether hate crimes from the left are as much a threat as those from the right, conservatives point to this series of unprovoked killings as proof they are correct.

Then there is the pressure from advocates for those who struggle with mental illness. With the ancient stereotype of "all persons with mental illness pose a threat and are dangerous" They are very eager to acknowledge that while the vast majority of those with mental illness are not dangerous, it is possible that sometimes, some mentally ill people do pose a threat.

It is proven however, that racial animus is an obsession, a symptom that only rears its head after the onset of paranoid schizophrenia. The suspect's mother told The Star that her son refused to get treatment for what she has long seen as his paranoid schizophrenia.

This would definitely be a poor defense for Scott, because "not guilty by reason of insanity" is rarely argued and almost never successful. Congress and half the states passed laws limiting the use of this defense. Now, the legal definition of insanity requires a break from reality that is so severe that the accused no longer knows what he is doing is wrong. This standard goes back to the mid-1800s.

Fifth victim: Steven Gibbons, aged 57, was shot in the back of the head as he walked along a south Kansas City street. Video surveillance shows Scott following him off a bus and down a south Kansas City street on August 13, 2017 and he was later seen running from the scene of Gibbons' murder. Gibbons was found in the 1100 block of East 67th Street and he was rushed to the hospital where he survived on life support for over a day before succumbing to his wounds and dying on August 14, 2017.

SCOTT'S COURT APPEARANCE:

A man suspected in five killing on or near south Kansas City trails has appeared in court, providing the victims' families a first chance to see him in person.

Several relatives dabbed their eyes as they left the courtroom. Afterward, Brian Darby, said, "We want justice." Scott is a suspect in the death of Darby's father, 61-year-old Mike Darby, but hasn't been charged in his killing. The police say, at this time, there is not enough evidence to connect and charge Scott with the other three murders.

The Kansas City Star reports that the court appearance Thursday for 22-year-old Fredrick Scott was brief. Prosecutors received a continuance in the case until Oct. 23 over the objections of Scott's public defender. Prosecutors announced last week that Scott had been charged in two killings and is a suspect in three more over nine months. All five were fatally shot, most from behind.

Police say they aren't sure if the murders were racially motivated, but say the accused told detectives he was upset about the 2015 shooting death of his half-brother. The killer was sentenced last week to 45 years in prison.

"Anyone who shoots innocent people walking on a trail should be prosecuted as heavily as possible," Shaton Duncan, who lives near the trail, told CBS affiliate KCTV.

These horrendous murders terrorized the community for months.

"I was in the Army overseas but I didn't want to walk on the trail by myself, that's how dangerous it felt," area resident Chuck Loomis told the station.

It has been an incredibly difficult six months for the family of David Lenox, but news of an arrest has them feeling more confident than ever they'll see justice for their father.

"Yesterday was very emotional with all the families. It was really hard for everyone," said Mindy Lenox.

Lenox and her brother Mike have lived in a true state of pure heartache for the last six months, endlessly working to keep their father's case in the spotlight.

They say while they didn't know exactly what Jackson County Prosecutor Jean Peters Baker would announce Tuesday, the fact investigators suggested Mindy catch a flight from San Francisco to Kansas City tipped them the news was substantial.

Frederick Scott has been charged with two of the murders along the trail - not with David Lenox's - but he is a suspect.

"Now that we have a name and a picture, anyone that knows Frederick Scott that may not have realized that it was vital information for the police," Lenox said. "If they could come forward, that's what we're looking for so that the remaining three families can receive justice as well."

The family says there is some relief just knowing there has been an arrest and that they can rest easier knowing that justice for David Lenox may only be a few tips away.

"I'm so pleased with the Kansas City Missouri Police Department," Michael Lenox said. "I can't thank them enough. Really just tremendous work on their part. They still got more work to do, but I'm very confident they'll get it done."

Since Tuesday's announcement, there have already been multiple tips called in. And anyone who thinks they might have any information at all is encouraged to call the tip line.

It was the Gibbons killing that led police to Scott, who had been mowing lawns to make money and, during the time of the shootings on the trails, had been working at a Burger King at Red Bridge and Holmes roads — within a few miles of three of the shooting scenes.

According to police in Kansas City, Scott did not own a car during the time of the killings, and got around town much of the time by walking. Also, Scott told investigators that he frequently used the Indian Creek Trail as a shortcut. He had a friend at the Willow Creek apartments near the trail. One of the victims was found shot and killed outside those homes. Other than walking, Scott told police that his primary mode of transportation was the public bus.

Allegedly, the bus is where Scott found Steven Gibbons.

Shortly after noon on Aug. 13, police were called to 1146 E. 67th Street, where officers found Gibbons shot in the back of the head.

Detectives found surveillance video that showed Gibbons, minutes before the shooting, boarding a KCATA bus at 75th Street and Troost Avenue. He was followed by a man carrying an iced tea bottle.

When Gibbons stepped off the bus at 67th Street, the man followed him, walking behind Gibbons closing the distance between them.

The surveillance camera panned away from the scene of the shooting, so detectives did not get a video record of the actual murder, but about 40 seconds later, the video showed the suspect running from the shooting scene and boarding a bus again.

Just west of the crime scene, detectives later found an iced tea bottle like the one in the video.

At a nearby gas station, detectives obtained video showing a man buying a bottle of iced tea just a few minutes before boarding the bus behind Gibbons.

Detectives took a still photo from that video and circulated it among police, who four days after the shooting matched the photo to

Scott, whom they found sitting on a wall and smoking a cigarette at 97th Street and Holmes.

Officers watched Scott throw the cigarette butt on the ground and then picked it up, sending it to the department's Regional Crime Lab for forensic testing. That same day, the lab matched the DNA on the cigarette butt to the iced tea bottle.

When police arrested Scott, he allegedly admitted shooting Gibbons but said it had been an accident – that he had been taking the gun out of his pocket when it went off.

While the motive in the killings remains unclear, Scott repeatedly told investigators that he was angry about the 2015 shooting death of his brother, Gerrod H. Woods, aged 23.

Woods was one of two men fatally shot Dec. 14, 2015 during a robbery near East 73rd Street and Wabash Avenue. On Friday, Jimmie Verge, the man convicted in those killings, was handed a 45-year prison sentence.

CONDOLENCES AND RELIEF FOR FAMILIES AND RESIDENTS

Jean Peters Baker said there was no clear motive in the killings. "To the families, there's no motive that makes sense. There just isn't," she said.

John Palmer's family has endured a difficult year since his death a year ago.

He left behind his wife, two grown children, two grandchildren and a large extended collection of family and friends.

Palmer was found shot several times, including in the back, on Aug. 19, 2016, near the Indian Creek Trail. His body had been dragged off the trail into some woods.

Police found a t-shirt at the scene with DNA that matched Scott — who, a year later, under arrest for the Gibbons killing, admitted killing Palmer, a man who relatives said liked to go on long walks through nature.

"He was walking love," said Janelle Kristian of Olathe, Palmer's first cousin. The two grew up in the same house as children. He was, she said, "a man of integrity, honesty and caring."

Palmer wasn't there for the gathering of some 65 people who always celebrate Thanksgiving together, Kristian said. It's been hard "knowing we won't see him again."

But there was solace, she said, when family members began sharing the news from the prosecutor's office, that someone had been arrested and charged.

"I feel glad to think maybe they have found and stopped who was doing this horrible thing," she said. "It's an awful thing to go through."

Kansas City Police Chief Rick Smith said at least 50 law enforcement personnel have worked on the investigation of the killings. The FBI assisted. On Tuesday, Smith said he extended his condolences to the families of the victims.

"We know this has been an incredibly painful and difficult time for each of you," Smith said. "We have worked diligently to bring the person responsible for these crimes to prosecution."

John Sharp, a former Kansas City council member who now leads the South Kansas City Alliance and was at the press conference Tuesday, said people living near the trails could be relieved to know a suspect has been arrested and charged.

"I think it will bring everybody peace of mind," Sharp said. "We had our south Kansas City Alliance problem-solving event on Saturday and a lady told me that how much she missed walking on the trails but her adult children wouldn't let her walk on them anymore.

"I think she wanted me to reassure her it was safe and of course I couldn't do it," he said. "But now I can."

At this point, everyone involved just hopes to continue to collect more tips and more evidence until they can finally solve the other three murders, whether or not that means convicting Scott of them. Were the killings racially motivated? Were they the result of a paranoid schizophrenic who had no professional help with the disease? Either way, they five victims are still gone, forever. We may never know the whole story behind these horrible events, but hopefully, they will be solved and justice will be served.

CHARLES MANSON'S HITMAN

AIMEE BAXTER

Charles Denton Watson was the pride of Copeville, Texas at one point. Nobody ever suspected that he would become "Tex" Watson, the "lieutenant for killing" in Charles Manson's horrifying "family." It had to come as quite a shock to all who knew him in that small north Texas community. It certainly shocked the world.

Everyone who knew him before must have wondered what happened...

What went so wrong in Charles Watson's life to take him from choirboy to killer? How did he become part of the horrible act that brought an end to the '60s? As Rolling Stone magazine said, "Their terror brought a halt to the peace and love of the 1960s."

Before He Met Manson

Born in Farmersville, Texas on December 2, 1945 and growing up in nearby Copeville, Charlie Watson was every parent's dream. The youngest of three children, Charlie attended Copeville Methodist Church where as a teen he led his church youth group and regularly attended Sunday evening service.

In high school, he was an honor roll student, star football player, and editor for the school paper. During his summers, he worked in an onion packing plant to save for college. He was the 1960s version of the all-American boy.

In September of 1964, Watson moved to Denton, Texas to attend North Texas State University where he joined a fraternity. His time at college was relatively uneventful. He studied, he partied, he dated ... standard college life.

His Junior year of college Charles Watson – now a 6 foot 2 inch 25 year old man – took a job as a baggage handler at Braniff Airlines. Through his job, he obtained free airline tickets and began to travel. On one trip, he flew out to Los Angeles, California to visit a fraternity buddy.

It was January 1967 and the psychedelic, music lifestyle was in full swing in LA. Watson became enthralled with the drug addled, free love lifestyle of the late 60s in California and decided to move out there.

He enrolled in California State but soon dropped out as he became more immersed in the "hippie" lifestyle. While cruising the California hills, Watson picked up a hitchhiker who turned out to be Beach Boy Dennis Wilson. To return Watson's kindness, Wilson invited him to his mansion to "chill."

Upon arriving, Watson found the mansion filled with people who were just hanging out, listening to music – from impromptu performances from various 'guests,' and doing lots and lots of drugs. Soon he moved in to join the various vagabonds living there besides Wilson.

It was there that Charles Manson's harem of girls lured him into Manson's web like the sirens of Greek mythology luring him to his doom. (And no, that is not being too dramatic.) When Wilson inevitably kicked everyone out, Watson naturally moved into the ranch where Manson and his 'family' where squatting, Spahn Ranch.

He moved out briefly at the end of fall in November of 1968 to live with a girlfriend. This relationship was short lived and he was back at the ranch by the spring of 1969. When he returned, he found that the focus of the "Manson Family" had morphed into what Manson called "Helter Skelter" which was his term for the inevitable race war he foresaw coming. Disillusioned with society, with a mind that had become drug addled and warped by the teachings of Manson Family "Guru" Charles Manson, "Tex" Watson, as he had become known by at the ranch, was primed and ready to stand as Manson's lieutenant.

The Tate Massacre

On a muggy August morning police are called to 10050 Cielo Drive in the posh area of Benedict Canyon in the Beverly Crest area just north of Beverly Hills. The caretaker for the home – currently being rented by director Roman Polanski and his pregnant girlfriend, actress Sharon Tate – had made a grisly discovery when arriving that morning for work.

According to Time Magazine, "The brutality of the killings shocked even homicide-squad detectives." Before they even entered the house, investigators found three bodies on the front lawn of the beautiful California mansion. To begin understanding what happened here, one must look to the evening before the horrifying discovery.

Instigating the Race War

Not long after Tex Watson returned to the commune the Manson Family had built at Spahn Ranch, Manson laid out his plan to "jump start" the race war he saw coming. On August 8, 1969, Tex Watson led Manson's 'army' into battle at the home at 10050 Cielo Drive.

It was at this home that Manson met with music producer Terry Melcher and where Melcher rejected Manson's attempts to get a music deal. According to testimony given by a Manson Family member who drove the car to the house in the Beverly Crest area, "Manson was angry with Melcher for not pursuing the deal and arrived at the latter's house at 10050 Cielo Drive to confront him. However, Melcher had moved on and the house was now occupied by Roman Polanski and Sharon Tate. Manson was told to leave."

"This residence - 10050 Cielo Drive - where Tate and Polanski now lived came to symbolize the establishment to Charles Manson, particularly the establishment's rejection of him," said Vincent Bugliosi, the District Attorney who prosecuted the case and later wrote the bestselling novel Helter Skelter. Believing that the race war he foresaw could be instigated, Manson devised a plan and the residents of the Cielo Drive mansion were to be unwitting, unwilling participants.

"Helter Skelter"

Together with Susan Adkins, Patricia "Katie" Krenwinkel, and driver Linda Kasabian, Tex Watson travelled the short distance to the large estate of Cielo Drive on the evening of August 8, 1969. Watson later said that Manson had given him and Krenwinkel orders to "kill every living thing."

Having been there previously on a scouting mission, Watson went first. He climbed a phone pole near the front gate, cut the phone wires to the house, and jumped over. The three women followed him.

In the driveway leading to the house, the four interlopers ran into 18-year-old Steven Parent who had been staying in the guesthouse and was driving out for a reason that no one will ever know. Watson charged the younger, smaller boy still in his car and while he pled for his life, cold bloodedly shot him with a .22 caliber Longhorn revolver five times at point blank range in the chest and abdomen.

Watson, Adkins, and Krenwinkel then pushed the boy's car further up the driveway to prevent it from being noticeable from the road. Driver Linda Kasabian returned to their car in shock, unable to continue with the plan. Later she is quoted as telling investigators, "I never really thought they were going to hurt anybody. Charlie (Manson) never told me we were going to kill people. I thought we were just going to freak them out & paint some messages on the walls to get our point out, you know. I never thought they were going to hurt anybody. Oh, God help me."

God, however, had no part in the events that transpired at the Polanski/Tate house.

After Watson cut a window screen, entered the home, and let his cohorts, Atkins and Krenwinkel, in through the front door. Although Polanski himself was in London filming, Sharon Tate and three friends were inside. Hairdresser Jay Sebring, writer Wojciech Frykowski, and Folger's coffee heiress Abigail Folger were all visiting with Tate that fateful day.

Watson admitted to directing the actions of the two women who were with him. At the time taking pride in his role as Manson's "Lieutenant of Death."

Watson found Sebring and Tate talking in her bedroom. He tied them together at the neck with a long rope. Meanwhile the two women held the home's other occupants in the living room area at gunpoint. Watson met them there, pulling a heavily pregnant Tate and Sebring out by the rope attached to their necks. A rope, which he quickly threw over a beam as if to hang them.

It was then that the real horror began. While not all of the details of what happened will ever truly be known, events that followed were not for the faint of heart. According to the pieced together accounts of the only three people to walk out of the Cielo Drive house that day, what followed sounds like a scene from one of the gory horror movies for which Tate was known.

When the teary and shaken prisoners asked the inevitable questions, who are you and what do you want, Watson answered them. "I'm the devil and I'm here to do the devil's business," he reportedly shouted and the women cheered him on.

Sebring resists being bound at the wrists and Watson shoots him without hesitation. The wound is not deadly however, and Sebring has more horror to endure.

With all four captives tied at the wrists, and Sebring and Tate still bound together at the necks, the three intruders pulled out the knives they had brought with them. It is speculated that this is the moment the four occupants realized they were not simply being robbed.

Like a swarm of locusts, the three fell on their victims with a maniacal glee. They stabbed wildly as their victims fought in vain with bound wrists to protect themselves.

At one point after the attack started, Folger and Frykowski bolted from the scene and were chased down in the front yard by Krenwinkel and Atkins. Frykowski took a shot to the leg before falling to the ground where Atkins fell upon him and finished him with multiple stabs to the chest and abdomen.

Already weak from the stabs she had endured inside, Folger was easily brought down by Krenwinkel who viciously pummeled her with stabs from her knife. She alone had over 28 stab wounds although, mercifully, coroners estimate that she was dead after only half of those stabs wounds were delivered.

Inside, Watson was left alone with Sebring and Tate. According to coroners, he finished off Sebring first with multiple stab wounds adding to the blood already lost through the bullet wound in his shoulder.

Then it was just him and eight month pregnant Tate.

The women returned as Watson was finishing off Tate. His brutality was something out of a nightmare. She pleaded with him to spare her baby's life, at one point – according to Krenwinkel – even asking him to cut the baby out of her before he killed her.

Tex Watson was merciless though and like any good soldier, follows his orders. He would leave not one person alive, even if they could not identify the three assailants.

"She was pleading to me and pleading to me, but I didn't even have a moment of hesitation. I took a knife and just slit a big slit across her face. And I just kept cutting her and carving on the body and started stabbing her in the chest— I'd say maybe 15 cuts and stabs. She was crying and saying, 'Oh mother, oh mother.' She said, 'Just let my baby live. You can kill me, but let my baby live.' I was actually the executioner."

These are the words of Tex Watson in 1978 describing what happened the night of the murders.

Once everyone was dead, the three used Sharon Tate's blood to write the messages Manson was sure would convince the attack was made by African American assailants. Scrawled across the walls and other surfaces were the words, "Die Pigs," "WAR," and "Helter Skelter."

The last was a recently released Beatles song. According to Manson, the Beatles were speaking in code to him and "Helter Skelter" was the term they used to describe the coming race war.

All told, over 102 separate stab wounds were found on the four victims. When police arrived, they found Steven Parent still in his car, Abigail Folger and Wojciech Frykowski sprawled on the front lawn where they had died, as well as Jay Sebring and Sharon Tate still bound together.

According to Time magazine, "Tate and Sebring had been repeatedly slashed. Bullets filled the ceilings and blood covered the floors. Tate was found naked, and [one] of Miss Tate's breasts had been cut off, apparently as a result of indiscriminate slashing. She was nine months pregnant, and there was an X cut on her stomach."

The horror for the peace touting, free loving mindset of the late '60s, however, was not done.

The LaBianca Murders

Upon returning to the Spahn Ranch, Watson and his cohorts reported directly to Manson. Their guru however was not happy. He felt they had bungled it. The next morning when the news came out, Manson's doubts were confirmed and he was livid.

"I remember him telling us we were all failures." Watson said in a jailhouse interview in 1982. "He kept telling us that we had put the entire plan at risk and that if we were destroyed with the white establishment it would be our own fault. At the time, that seemed like the worst thing in the world to me."

Manson gave them a chance to redeem themselves the following night, August 9. With Linda Kasabian acting as driver again, Manson gathered Watson and his two cohorts from the night before, Susan Atkins and "Katie" Krenwinkel. Adding two new "family" members to the group, Leslie VanHouten and Steve "Clem" Grogan, Manson intended to "show them how it is done."

Manson wanted to target Harold True with this attack but felt that it might be traced back to him because in March of 1968 he and some of his "family" members attended a party at True's home in the Los Feliz-Griffith Park area of Los Angeles. He settled instead for the house next door at 3301 Waverly Drive. The home of Leno and Rosemary LaBianca.

After driving past the house repeatedly, they parked just down the street and Watson got out with Manson. According to Watson's book *Will You Die for Me*, he and Manson entered the house while the women waited and Manson held the occupants at gunpoint while he tied them up. Manson then returned to the car after telling Watson, "You know what needs to be done. Do it right this time."

He sent Krenwinkel and VanHouten into the house to assist Watson and the terror began. The girls took Rosemary into her bedroom while Watson stayed with Leno in the den. There was no hesitation, no playing around this time around. Watson murdered Leno by stabbing him to death in the den then joined the girls in Rosemary's bedroom.

With VanHouten unable to bring herself to actually plunge her knife into Rosemary, Watson says he and Krenwinkel finished the woman off together. During the investigation, he even came to VanHouten's defense saying, "Leslie shouldn't be charged with anything. She couldn't do it. She just sat there kind of freaking out, you know. I dripped some blood from my knife onto hers while I was trying to get her to do it but she wouldn't, you know."

Before leaving the house, Krenwinkel wrote the words "WAR," "Helter Skelter," "RISE," and "Death to PIGS" on the walls and other surfaces in the LaBianca's blood. As an afterthought, Watson carved the word "WAR" into Leno LaBianca's stomach and stabbed a fork into it. They hoped that the messages would make detectives with the Los Angeles Police Department link this killing to that from the day before and finally blame the black community as Manson had hoped.

One Last Murder Before You Go

When that did not happen, the Manson Family began to dissolve. When attention turned to them, Manson had one last murder for Tex Watson before he left that of Donald "Shorty" Shea. A ranch hand at the Spahn Ranch, Manson felt it was he who had tipped off the Los Angeles Police Department.

Running Home

Once the attention of the LAPD began to turn to the group at Spahn Ranch, in early October of '69, Tex Watson to the only other place he had ever really known. Charles "Tex" Watson ran home to Texas.

It was there in McKinley, Texas that the law caught up to him on November 30, 1969. After starting a normal life in the small Texas community, the guy that had become known as Charlie to his new friends was exposed for who he really was, the soulless fiend behind the horrendous events that had been gripping the headlines for months.

Watson and his attorneys in Texas fought extradition back to California for nine months but eventually lost. In August of 1970, a full year after the horrendous murders, Tex Watson returned to face justice.

However, upon returning to California, he stopped eating and talking and began regressing into a catatonic state. He lost 55 pounds and was admitted to Atascadero State Hospital for a 90-day evaluation period to determine if he was fit to stand trial.

Although his 90-day period was up in November of 1970, it was not until February of 1971 until he was deemed able to stand trial. Less sensational than the group trial of Charles Manson and the other members of his "family," Charles "Tex" Watson's trial ended on October 12, 1971.

On that date, he was found guilty of seven counts of first-degree murder and of seven counts of conspiracy to commit murder. One count each for Sharon Tate, Wojciech Frykowski, Steven Parent, Sharon Tate, Jay Sebring, Leno LaBianca, and Rosemary LaBianca. He was not charged or tried in the death of the ranch hand Shea, as it was not known of until later.

A week later, the same jury took only two and a half hours to decide that Watson was sane. He was sentenced to death.

Luckily, for him, the case of People vs. Anderson caused the California Supreme Court to decide that all death sentences handed down prior to 1972 were invalid. His sentence was converted to life in prison.

Prison

Because Watson's life sentences were to be served concurrently, it made him eligible for parole on November 26, 1976. Had he been granted parole at his first opportunity, Charles "Tex" Watson would have served only one year for each of the people he was convicted of murdering. He was not paroled however, and would spend many years behind bars at the Mule Creek State Prison in Ione, California.

In 1975, Charles Watson – as he asked that the "Tex" be dropped at this time – converted to Christianity. Then in 1978, his autobiography as it was told to the man known as Chaplin Ray, Ray Hoekstra, was published. It was titled Will You Die for Me and his name was once again a household name.

In 1979, Kristin Joan Svege began writing to Watson in prison after reading his book. They were married in September of that same year and soon began having conjugal visits.

Psychologists still use Kristin Joan Svege as an example of hybristophilia. This is defined by Psychology.com as "a sexual paraphilia in which an individual derives sexual arousal and pleasure from having a sexual partner who is known to have committed an outrage or crime such as rape, murder, or grand theft." Essentially, the term used to describe why people fall in love with criminals who have committed crimes that horrify others. The ultimate Bad Boy complex.

In 1980, Charles Watson became a first time. His son, named Joshua after the biblical man of the same name, was born without the usual fanfare associated with a first child. This was done, in part, to keep the press from finding out.

In 1981, he became an ordained minister and wrote letters to Doris Tate, Sharon's mother, asking for forgiveness. She responded by doubling her efforts to make sure that he was never released on parole.

She was not the only one who wanted to see Watson kept behind bars. In August of 1982, a southern California based group known as Citizens for Truth submitted over 80,000 petition signatures and several 1000 letters opposing his parole. It was again denied. Watson is known to have complained loudly and often about the efforts to keep him incarcerated.

Later that year his second son with Svege was born. Two more followed closely after that. Now Watson had a wife, three sons, and a daughter waiting on the outside for him.

Yet his parole was repeatedly thwarted by the continued efforts of Doris Tate and her other two daughters, Patricia and Debra. Together, they submitted over two million signatures to keep Watson in prison for the rest of his life.

In 1992, Doris Tate died knowing she had done all that she could to keep her daughter and unborn grandson's murderer in prison for the rest of his life

In October of 1996, the state of California officially banned conjugal visits for inmates. Individuals and groups alike had strongly opposed them for years arguing that it was unfair to the children that inmates had the opportunity to father while incarcerated, some for life.

In 2003, Svege divorced Watson when she met a man on the outside and fell in love. According to Watson, they remained friends for years afterwards and she always brought the kids for Father's Day. Records from the prison however indicate that Svege stopped bringing the children to visit in 2000.

During this time, Watson began a prison outreach website for his Amazing Love Ministries. His mission statement said that he hoped to help inmates who found their way to God while behind bars keep on that straight and narrow path after their release.

In 2012, Charles Watson became part of another court case. Although, this time not as a defendant. After his attorney's death, the recorded meetings between him and Charles Watson became part of a bankruptcy proceeding involving the deceased attorney's law firm. Watson disputed their release.

Members of the LAPD chimed in saying that they believed the recordings might contain clues about unsolved murder cases involving the Manson Family. Watson asked the presiding judge to allow police to listen to the tapes but not to give the Los Angeles Police Department possession of them.

Eventually, the LAPD won out and the tapes were given into their possession. The tapes allegedly contain Watson confessing to other murders but according to the official record, they "did not contain any new information."

In 2013, an "unidentified" inmate stabbed Watson in the back several times and attempted to throw him off a second tier balcony.

According to Watson's testimony at a February 2016 parole hearing, he was washing his clothes in a sink on the second tier when another inmate that he did not recognize began hovering around him. Watson says that he did not think the man was a threat due to his small stature. He noticed that the man had a rolled up magazine but thought nothing of it at the time.

The inmate then asked Watson if he knew anything about Kabala. Watson says that he answered the man "No" and began walking away from him. That is when the inmate began stabbing him in the back with a sharpened paintbrush. "I thought he was just punching me," said Watson in his parole hearing. "I didn't realize I was stabbed until he tried to lift me over the railing."

Prison records support Watson's account of the events but do not identify the assailant.

Many of the comments on CieloDrive.com where this report was posted in 2016 were anything but sympathetic with many professing that Watson "got what he deserved." According to the statement he made at his parole hearing that same year, Watson agrees with those sentiments. "It is kind of ironic isn't it? I guess I deserved it."

Conclusion

In the 40 plus years since he first became eligible for parole, Charles Denton Watson, serial killer, "Lieutenant of Death," ordained minister, and divorced father of four has been denied freedom 17 times. The last of which was a five year denial given to him on October 27, 2016.

At that time, he was 70 years old.

It is unlikely that Watson will ever see life outside the walls of Mule Creek State Prison again. If he does, he will be 75 years old.

SWEDEN'S SERIAL KILLER

ANA BENSON

115

Sometimes the truth is stranger than fiction. This sentence really describes the case of Sture Bergwall, a Swedish man who was once considered the most prolific serial killer in that country. But after another shocking turn of events, he became an example of someone who was completely wronged by the system.

The life of Sture Bergwall is a rollercoaster. He started off as an intelligent young man who had an interest in art and drama even though he lived in a small town. Unfortunately, his addiction to drugs turned him into a criminal. After that, he became known throughout the Europe as Sweden's most dangerous killer after he confessed to thirty cold cases which spanned throughout the decades.

But he did eventually come clean and claimed that every single story he told was a lie. Sture Bergwall, also known as Thomas Quick is now a free man, and his story sounds like something out of a detective novel set in a far corner of Northern Europe.

Early life

Sture Ragnar Bergwall was born on April 26th, 1950 in Korsnäs which is located in Sweden. It is a rural town where nothing interesting happens. He had six siblings, including a twin sister. They were somewhat close, and his sister would later describe him as completely different from the rest of the family. She suspected that he suffered a brain injury while he was at a hospital recovering from tuberculosis. As a matter of fact, he was only seven years old when he contracted the illness and he came back home a year later.

Bergwall was always prone to accidents and another one happened while he was in his early teens. He was playing with his brothers when he stumbled and fell into a gravel pit, hitting his head pretty hard. There was an iron pipe at the bottom of the hole, and Bergwall ran straight into it. The impact was so hard that he felt nauseous right away and started vomiting on the spot. From this moment on he became a different person.

It is hard to say what is true when it comes to Bergwall's childhood, especially if you focus on his initial confessions only. Bergwall himself would say that he grew up in an abusive environment with a father who sexually abused him until he hit puberty and a mother who would beat him on a regular basis. His parents were very religious, and they were a part of the Pentecostal church. Having in mind that Sture Bergwall realized he was a homosexual when he was fourteen, it is clear that his childhood was not easy, especially due to the fact that being queer was not something that was readily acceptable back then.

He clearly stated in his interviews from the 1990s that one of his first memories was when he was only four years old and his father was abusing him. Bergwall's mother walked in the room, saw what was going on, and had a miscarriage right there on the spot. His father showed him the body of his stillborn baby brother who was seven months old and that moment became imprinted forever into Bergwall's mind.

His mother started blaming Bergwall for the miscarriage, so she tried to kill him several times. Winters in Sweden are particularly harsh, and she attempted to drown him in a frozen lake soon after the incident. His mother also tried to push him into traffic. According to initial statements made by Bergwall, the abuse he suffered as a child distorted his views on what is right and what is wrong when it comes to sexuality. So he became interested in younger boys while he was a teenager himself.

His twin sister confirms that she did hear her parents say that Bergwall was indeed abusing fellow schoolmates and that the children welfare was involved in the situation as well. Bergwall did describe the incidents in detail while he was interviewed by the police in the 1990s, and would say that it was called *The Strangulation Game*. He would go to the showers with his classmates, put his arm around one's neck, and touch his genital area with a free hand. Bergwall did not think it would be considered abuse and he saw it as natural curiosity regarding human body since he was only twelve at the time.

According to Bergwall, he met a man who was in his twenties and the two became really close friends. The said man loved to drive around and meet younger boys which did partially explain why he apparently befriended Bergwall. They really liked each other, so the unnamed man invited Bergwall to accompany him on the long drives. Bergwall became the one who would talk to the boys first, inviting them to the man's car where they would be eventually molested. He would take part in the abuse sometimes while the man watched and touched himself. Bergwall was only fourteen years old when this was allegedly happening.

The first murder?

During the time Bergwall spent driving around with the unnamed man, the two of them visited an amusement park. It was a weekend, and the park did have a large number of visitors. Bergwall met a boy who was around his own age. His name was Thomas Blomgren, and they struck a conversation right away. After spending hours and hours wandering around, Bergwall suggested that they should explore the nearby woods. When they reached a fairly secluded place, Bergwall attacked the boy, strangling him to death. His first murder was closely linked to the so-called *Strangulation Game* he had played in school because after he murdered Blomgren with his bare hands, Bergwall proceeded to touch his genitals.

Bergwall left Blomgren's body in the woods and set out to find the man who was his ride back home. Once they were in the car, Bergwall told him what he had done, and the man promised he would never tell on him. This event apparently strengthened the bond they shared. But of course, according to his confessions, this wasn't the end of Bergwall's murderous urges. As a matter of fact, Bergwall found his next victim one year later, but the incident was ruled out as an accidental drowning. Bergwall was hanging out by Lake Åsnen when he saw a thirteen-year old boy Alvar Larsson on the shore. He snuck up to the boy and pushed him into the water. The boy was quickly pulled under, and he drowned. Since there were no witnesses, the authorities were certain that the boy slipped, and fell into the lake. No one had any suspicions about a second person being involved.

The time went by, and according to Bergwall, he was laying low. Recreational drug use became his new hobby, and he was addicted to amphetamines at that time. According to his confessions, he was managing to suppress his homicidal thoughts during this time. He was sent to a rehab facility when his parents found out about the drugs he was taking. Bergwall would say that he befriended and killed a boy who was staying with him in the rehab. These claims were never confirmed by the law enforcement or the staff who worked at the rehab clinic. He was released a couple of months later and was in search of a job. Bergwall ended up working as a medic which supposedly gave him access to potential victims. Even though he was doing his best not to be discovered, Bergwall did try to strangle another boy who was staying at the hospital. He stopped before it was too late and felt terrible afterward.

Bergwall thought that a confession to a priest would relieve his consciousness, so he visited a church soon after this incident. Yes, no one was hurt, but the priest called the police and told them about the attempted murder. They brought him to the police station and did a psychological evaluation which revealed that he was a deeply disturbed individual. He was placed in a psychiatric hospital and Bergwall spent the next three years of his life locked away from the society.

This didn't mean that the people around him were safe because according to his later confessions, the security measures in the psych ward were almost non-existent and he was able to get away with many things, including the murder. Bergwall claimed that he strangled another patient, and the staff did not manage to prevent this. Bergwall also told the authorities that he was free to walk out of the psychiatric hospital whenever he wanted. His story was that the security did not even try to stop him. This is highly unlikely because psychiatric hospitals do have high-security measures.

Getting caught and the series of confessions

Everything will start unraveling in 1990 when Bergwall tried to rob a bank with his 16-years old accomplice. They created a large commotion by taking the bank manager's family as hostages. The duo needed money to buy drugs, so they were ready to do anything. The police intervened, and both of them were arrested. Bergwall ended up in prison that specialized in criminally insane inmates. And this is where he started confessing to his crimes. He also dropped the name Sture Bergwall and decided to call himself Thomas Quick. As you might recall, Thomas was the name of his alleged first victim. Quick was his mother's maiden name.

Bergwall who was now called Quick started attending therapy sessions which were a part of his rehabilitation program. He openly talked to his therapist about the crimes he had committed, and that number slowly grew. The therapist who was in charge contacted the police, and they started interviewing Bergwall after each and every session. The detectives were taking notes, and building a case surrounding Bergwall. Some of his claims seemed almost impossible because he was confessing to so many cold cases which were gathering up dust on police shelves for years. Some of the murders were quite old, and the police were unable to present them during the trials because the statute of limitations has expired.

One thing was immediately strange to the outside critics of the Swedish police, and that was the fact that there wasn't any physical evidence that would link Bergwall to the murders. As a matter of fact, each session was based solely on recovered memory therapy methods which did seem factual back then. However, recent studies did show that this type of treatment is not 100% certain, and some patients create false memories which lead to many inconsistencies. Since

Bergwall was unable to provide all the information about the murders, his therapist stated that his mind buried down the memories because they were simply too much to process.

Bergwall's therapist included benzodiazepines which were supposed to help him clear up his mind and relax. This was a wrong move because the doctors failed to acknowledge Bergwall's history of substance abuse. Some experts would say that there is a possibility that these medications triggered some sort of hallucinations which made Bergwall believe in his fabricated memories. But the truth was completely different, and it would be revealed decades later.

His testimonies were believable to the law enforcement back in the 1990s, and Bergwall quickly became Sweden's most prolific serial killer. The body count of his alleged victims grew after each and every therapy session. It did seem impossible that he knew so many details about unsolved murders, but there were many mistakes which were often disregarded by the interrogators who would continue to feed him information during the post therapy interviews. He could give the general description of a crime, but he was murky about the details. Whenever Bergwall got stuck, he would read the detective's facial expressions and try to come up with an acceptable answer. Some police officers did think that since he had many victims, he was starting to mix them up.

In the end, Bergwall confessed to around thirty murders. They were committed all over Scandinavia which included Sweden, Norway, Denmark, and Finland. It did sound a bit far-fetched, and critics started emerging right away, claiming that the police is abusing a mentally unstable person. One of them was an investigator who worked on a case to which Bergwall confessed. But since Bergwall claimed that he committed the first crime when he was only fourteen years old, the law enforcement apparently believed in his testimonies and proceeded to place Bergwall in front of a judge.

The trials

Sture Bergwall went through a total of six trials, starting in 1994 with the last one held in 2001. The majority of the murders he apparently committed were old, and there was no possibility for him to stand a trial for each and every one of them. Bergwall's defense was led by Claes Borgström, a well-known Swedish lawyer, and politician. He failed to see through Bergwall's false confessions and did a poor job of defending his client.

The first trial focused on the murder of Charles Zelmanovits who disappeared in 1976 in Piteå. The partial remains were found in 1993, but since the body was completely decomposed, the forensic experts were unable to tell exactly what happened to Zelmanovits. The detectives accepted Bergwall's version of the story, and the whole case relied solely on his testimony. He was found guilty without a single proof that he was even there when the murder occurred.

Then there were Marinus and Janni Stegehuis, a couple of Dutch tourists who were visiting Sweden in the summer of 1984. They camped by a lake near Appojaure. The couple wanted privacy, so they set up their tent in a secluded place. Other visitors to the camp site would find their bodies a day later. Both of them were brutally stabbed to death, possibly while they were sleeping. Other campers did see a suspicious looking man on the evening when the murders happened. He was covered in blood which did scare everyone who noticed him walking by the lake.

He was identified and questioned by the police, but claimed that he was a hunter and that the blood came from a deer. Eventually, Bergwall confessed to the killings which derailed the investigation. Once again, the investigators couldn't place Bergwall at the scene of the crime, but he did give them some details which were not released to the public. He was found guilty of the murder of the Stegehuis couple in 1996.

Another sentencing came in 1997, and this time it was for the murder of Yenon Levi who was an Israeli tourist traveling through Scandinavian countries. He was killed in 1988. Bergwall gave the investigators his statements about the murder, but there were too many inconsistencies. He couldn't even recall the right murder weapon. Levi was beaten with a wooden club, but Bergwall insisted that he used an axe. After a couple of tries and suggestions made by the police, he did confirm that he killed Levi with a blunt object. The defense did mention that Bergwall struggled a lot with this confession which should have told the judge that he fabricated the entire story. However, Bergwall was found guilty at the end of the proceedings.

Bergwall was on trial for the disappearance of Therese Johannesen in 1998. She was a nine-years old girl from Norway who vanished in 1988. Bergwall did provide the law enforcement with correct details of the abduction, but it would be later discovered that he managed to get his hands on the articles which covered this mysterious disappearance from a news crew who interviewed him while he was in prison. Bergwall claimed that he abducted the girl and then killed her. The only evidence was a bone fragment which supposedly belonged to Therese Johannesen. It would be revealed that no one took time to test the remains and that there were actually made of wood. Not to forget that there was absolutely no proof that Bergwall was even in Norway in the summer of 1988.

Trine Jensen was killed in Oslo in 1981, while Gry Storvik was murdered in the same city four years later. Bergwall included both of these crimes into his confessions, but there was no evidence that could link him to either of the crimes. As a matter of fact, the semen found on Storvik did not match Bergwall's DNA. This didn't stop the judge to find Bergwall guilty in 2000.

And finally, the last trial was centered on one of the most famous criminal cases in the history of Sweden – the disappearance of Johan Asplund. Even though this was the first murder Bergwall talked about during his therapy sessions, it took the investigators nine years to get enough material that can be presented in front of a judge. They couldn't uncover any actual evidence, but they went to the trial in spite of that.

Asplund disappeared when he was on his way to school in November of 1980. He was eleven years old, and his alleged kidnapping launched a huge investigation. Unfortunately, the law enforcement couldn't find the boy or his remains.

Bergwall told his psychiatrist that he waited in front of Asplund's school and then invited the boy in his vehicle. He drove him to the nearby woods where he sexually assaulted Asplund. Once he realized what he did, Bergwall strangled the boy and cut him into pieces. He hid them near the said woods. Bergwall did provide the police with the location of the buried remains, and they headed out in order to find the missing boy. The officers dug through the whole area but their efforts produced nothing. They still had no proof that Bergwall was telling the truth. But regardless of this, Bergwall was found guilty.

The critics and the doubt

As soon as the media started reporting on Bergwall back in 1993, there were a lot of skeptics who did not believe in his confessions. After all, he claimed that he had murdered somewhere around thirty people, but there were absolutely no witnesses or data that could confirm that he was even present at a scene of a single crime. Having in mind that the alleged murders occurred in several countries, it is hard to believe that there wouldn't be any information about his whereabouts.

The tales of alibies and mismatched DNA started appearing in the news, so more and more people started to realize the fact that Sture Bergwall wasn't the boogeyman, but a person with a serious mental illness who simply confessed to a large number of cold cases. If you might recall, Bergwall claimed that his first murder victim was a boy called Thomas Blomgren. Bergwall's own sister debunked this confession by telling the investigators that her brother couldn't have killed the boy since he was actually at their church with the entire family on the day of the murder. Bergwall's confirmation was held on that particular date.

The family members of the murder victims were not satisfied with the trials because they felt like the real killers were out there somewhere. After all, there wasn't a single piece of evidence that could prove that Bergwall killed anyone. If the police did find DNA samples on a victim, they did not match Bergwall's. Yes, it is strange why that didn't raise any red flags among the leading investigators back in the day, but the weirdest thing is that there were more than ten thousand witnesses who were questioned regarding these cases. None of them ever saw Bergwall. It seemed like he had the ability to simply vanish from a scene of a crime which is highly unlikely.

Forensic experts who had worked with the serial killers gave their opinion on Bergwall and stated that he did not match any murderer they had encountered before. He had no clear modus operandi, and according to his own testimonies, he would kill random victims. Murderers are known to have a certain type, but Bergwall didn't care about age, gender, or physical appearance. As a matter of fact, they could only compare him to Henry Lee Lucas, who was known for his fabricated confessions. It was obvious to everyone except the law enforcement that they made a huge mistake.

Bergwall himself attacked the media and the critics in his article which was published in *Dagens Nyheter*. He refused to give the police any additional information about the murders. This meant that his series of confessions was over. He returned to the public's eye in 2006 when a team of lawyers who were hired by some of the victims' parents asked for a case review from the Swedish Chancellor of Justice. They had proof which showed how the entire investigation was conducted poorly, and that Bergwall was mentally ill. These lawyers were backed up by Leif G. W. Persson, a famous criminologist. He was sure that Sture Bergwall was not a killer but a victim of the judicial system that wanted to close the cold cases regardless of who took the blame.

A large number of people believed that Bergwall was not telling the truth while others couldn't understand that someone would confess to a series of murders they didn't commit. So they continued to see him as a ruthless killer who terrorized Scandinavia over several past decades. But everything will soon change.

The actual truth

Sture Bergwall agreed to do a TV interview in 2008. It was supposed to be used for a documentary which described Bergwall's life, but the producers were intrigued when they realized that Bergwall was telling a whole new story. That video footage was the first step that led Bergwall to freedom. Soon after the cameras stopped rolling, Bergwall hired a new lawyer - Thomas Olsson. Olsson was familiar with the case and was ready to listen to Bergwall.

After everything he had heard regarding the confessions, the medications, and Bergwall's own history of drug abuse, Olsson was completely certain that Bergwall was not a murderer and that he should be set free. He would later say: "He is not dangerous at all! I don't like people too much in general. But, of course, if you spend so much time with a client, you always see the person behind the headlines. It all starts with a little boy under a Christmas tree, playing with toys and it ends up very tragic. Somewhere along the line, everyone is a victim."

Olsson dug deep into the procedures of the cases and did a thorough research even though there were a lot of paperwork that covered each and every trial. He discovered plenty of irregularities and omitted evidence that was not disclosed to all sides. One of the crucial things that were never told to the judge was the usage of benzodiazepines during Bergwall's therapy sessions. This evidence alone was enough to completely throw out each conviction. Bergwall did admit that he made up the stories in order to get more drugs and to be taken seriously in a facility where he was being kept back then.

Sture Bergwall asked the Svea Court of Appeal to grant him a new trial for the murder of Yenon Levi, and once it was approved, the ball started rolling. The new trial was scheduled for the winter of 2009.

Olsson told the new judge about the interview with the police and the fact that his client did not know the exact murder weapon. As a matter of fact, he was coerced or led to the correct answer by the police officers who were present in the interrogation room. Bergwall was cleared of any suspicion, and judge's initial ruling was thrown out.

The next step was the case of Therese Johannesen. Bergwall's new lawyer had enough proof to claim that his client had an alibi for the day of the disappearance. The charges were dropped soon after. Olsson did plan to appeal to every single conviction, but the prosecution knew that the entire case was falling apart. Sture Bergwall was cleared of all charges in 2013. He left the Säter's institution for the criminally insane under the condition that he attends therapy.

Bergwall passed his psychological examination after the release, and it showed that there was no need for him to continue to use his medication. The case of Sture Bergwall is a proof how an innocent man can be accused of heinous crimes because the system wants to believe in his guilt. There were plenty of opportunities to put an end to the madness, but the police did nothing. This man did spend a large portion of his life behind the bars, and he will never get that time back. But he did receive the justice he deserved, and hopefully, those cold cases he confessed to will be solved as well.

TED BUNDY

Ted Bundy is one of the most prolific serial killers of the 20th century, having kidnapped, raped, and murdered at least 36 attractive young women between 1973 and 1978 in Colorado, Oregon, Utah, Florida, and Washington; however, many assert that this figure could be much higher. He had also kept some of his victims' body parts—including heads—as trophies in a utility shed behind his Utah home, as well having engaged in necrophilia with decomposing corpses which he would groom and apply makeup.

A master manipulator and classic antisocial personality, Bundy escaped custody twice; once from court during his first murder trial and the second time from the Garfield County Jail in Colorado by sawing a hole in his cell ceiling. He was placed on the FBI's Ten Most Wanted list and was later arrested in Florida in February 1978 after stealing a car. He was sentenced to death in 1979 for the murder of two Florida State University sorority sisters, and again in 1980 for another murder.

Very charismatic and handsome, Bundy exploited these characteristics heavily with his young female victims in an effort to earn their sympathy trust. He would often approach potential victims in public places, feigning injury or impersonating an authority figure before overpowering them—usually by hitting them in the head with a crowbar—taking them to secluded locations, and raping and murdering them. Sometimes he would simply break into young women's homes and bludgeon them while they slept.

Bundy was originally incarcerated for aggravated kidnapping and attempted assault in 1975 in Utah; however, his list of homicide victims continued to grow. He escaped from custody twice in Colorado and subsequently committed three more murders before finally being apprehended in Florida in 1978. Ted Bundy was sentenced to death and was executed in the electric chair at Raiford Prison in Starke, Florida, on 24 January 1989.

Early Life

Theodore Robert Bundy—originally Theodore Robert Cowell—was born on 24 November 1946 at the Elizabeth Lund Home for Unwed Mothers in Burlington, Vermont. The social stigma of being a single mother was great at that time so Bundy's mother, Louise Cowell, took her infant son to live with her parents—Samuel and Eleanor—in Philadelphia where young Ted took on the Cowell surname and was told that they were, in fact, his parents and that his mother was his sister. Eventually, Bundy discovered the truth and harbored lifelong resentment toward his mother for lying to him.

Bundy's paternity has never been definitively proven. His birth certificate lists his father as Lloyd Marshall, an Air Force veteran and salesman; however, Louise has claimed that she was "seduced by 'a sailor'" whose name "may have been Jack Worthington" but nobody by that name was ever found in Navy or merchant marines records. Compounding the problem is that Bundy's grandfather, Samuel Cowell, has been rumored to be his biological father; thus making Bundy the product of incest; however, again, there is no evidence of this.

In interviews, Bundy spoke highly of his grandparents, especially expressing a fondness for his grandfather even though other family members described Samuel as a tyrannical bully and bigot who beat his wife and dog, abused his daughters, harmed neighborhood cats, and would sometimes "speak aloud to unseen presences". Bundy's grandmother was timid and obedient and was treated for her depression with electroconvulsive therapy.

Bundy exhibited disturbing behavior from a young age. At the age of three, he was alleged to have surrounded his sleeping aunt, Julia, with household knives—blades pointed toward her—and smiled at her when she had awakened.

In 1950, when Bundy was only four, Louise changed both her and her son's surname to Nelson and moved them both to Tacoma, Washington, to live with cousins Jane and Alan Scott. In 1951, Louise met hospital cook Johnny Culpepper Bundy at a church singles night and they married later that year. Johnny formally adopted young Ted and he adopted the last name of Bundy. Even with efforts to include young Ted in family activities along with his four half-siblings—who he was often left to babysit—he always was distant. Later, Bundy would tell his girlfriend that Johnny wasn't his real dad, wasn't smart enough, and didn't make much money.

Bundy confessed that he "chose to be alone" as an adolescent and neither had any natural inclination to develop any close friendships nor knew what drove people to be friends in the first place. He would later say that he "hit a wall" and his inability to comprehend social behavior stunted his social development, rendering him required to adopt a façade of social activity. He was terribly shy, self-doubting, and uncomfortable in social situations and often teased for being different. Despite this, he was a good student at Woodrow Wilson High School, was active in a local Methodist church, and was even involved with a local Boy Scout troop.

Bundy would also admit—while on death row—that a part of him as a young child was "fascinated by images of sex and violence" and he called this part "the entity". He enjoyed reading crime books and detective magazines, particularly those that contained descriptions of sexual violence and pictures of dead bodies. Later, before his execution, he would admit that pornography was central in shaping who he was.

Throughout high school Bundy loved to ski and was very good at it; however, his pursuit of this hobby was usually accomplished with stolen equipment and forged lift tickets. He was also arrested on at least two occasions on suspicion of auto theft and burglary but when he turned 18 his juvenile record was expunged. Stealing, for Bundy, did not involve any guilt and, in fact, he had a sense of entitlement about the entire thing. He often said that the thrill of taking possession of something he wanted without remorse was exciting. Many speculate that his "taking" of his victims represented this same concept and provided him with the same rush. Compounding the problem was his sense of entitlement and cunning ability to lie about everything which demonstrates a common trait among psychopaths.

Bundy graduated high school in 1965 and was awarded a scholarship by the University of Puget Sound where he started that fall, taking courses in Oriental studies and psychology. After two semesters he transferred to the University of Washington in Seattle.

He obtained employment as a stock boy and bagger at a Safeway store on Queen Anne Hill, in addition to other odd jobs. As part of his psychology curricula, he would work as a night-shift volunteer at Seattle's Suicide Hot Line where he met and worked Ann Rule who would later become among the world's foremost true crime writers and who penned a biography about Bundy—that was also partly autobiographical about her working relationship with him—entitled *The Stranger Beside Me* (1980).

While in college, circa 1968, Bundy began a relationship with fellow student "Stephanie Brooks" (a pseudonym); however, after she graduated in 1968 and prepared to move back home to California she broke up with Bundy due to what she described as his lack of ambition and immaturity. Bundy was heartbroken after this and, interestingly, all of his victims bore some resemblance to Brooks; particularly the fact that Brooks and all of his victims had long dark hair which they wore parted down the middle.

Shortly thereafter, Bundy returned to Burlington—his birthplace—and learned the truth of his parentage. This discovery made him more dominant and focused.

He managed the Seattle office of Nelson Rockefeller's presidential campaign in 1968 and attended the 1968 Republican convention in Miami, Florida. He reenrolled at the University of Washington with a major in psychology. He became popular among his professors as he was an honor student and also began a relationship with Elizabeth Kloepfer in 1969. Kloepfer was a divorced secretary with a young daughter and the two dated for the next six years until he went to prison in 1976.

Bundy graduated in 1972 with a degree in psychology and went to work for the state Republican Party.

In the fall of 1973, Bundy enrolled in the University of Utah Law School but did poorly because of poor attendance and, consequently, dropped out the following spring.

While in California on a business trip in the summer of 1973, Bundy found his ex-girlfriend "Stephanie Brooks" and the change in his look and attitude was appealing to her. Bundy courted Brooks the rest of the year—while still involved with Kloepfer—and proposed to her, only to dump Brooks shortly after the new year, likely in retaliation for her breaking his heart years earlier. The breakup wreaked havoc on Bundy who became obsessed with her and this obsession "would span his lifetime and lead to a series of events that would shock the world".

Mere weeks later, Bundy began his first murderous rampage in Washington; however, many Bundy experts assert that he likely starting killing in his teens. One case involved eight-year-old Ann Marie Burr from Tacoma who disappeared from her home in 1961 when Bundy was 14. Burr's house was on Bundy's newspaper delivery route and her father was positive that he saw Bundy near a construction site ditch on the nearby University of Puget Sound campus the day his daughter vanished. Despite other potentially incriminating circumstantial evidence, Bundy remains merely a suspect due to a lack of consensus by law enforcement personnel as to whether they believe he actually did it or not. Bundy has always denied killing her.

Shortly before his execution, Bundy did, in fact, tell his attorney that his first attempt at kidnapping was in 1969 and his first "actual murder" occurred "sometime in 1972". While he was a suspect in the December 1973 murder of Kathy Devine in Washington, DNA analysis exonerated him and her true murderer was convicted in 2002.

Bundy's earliest identified murders were committed in 1974 when he was 27.

Bundy was a handsome and charismatic guy, particularly to his young female victims and he exploited these characteristics fully. He was also an adept chameleon, able to blend in and feign belonging which increased his threat to the attractive brunette women he targeted as his victims. This charm and his adroitness at lying and manipulation made him extremely dangerous.

Known Murder Victims

Karen Sparks (often referred to as Joni Lenz), 18 (survived)

On 4 January 1974, 18-year-old Karen Sparks/Joni Lenz was found by her roommates when she didn't emerge from her bedroom that morning. They were not prepared for what horrific sights they saw. Sparks had been beaten badly and a bed rod ripped from the bed was "savagely rammed into her vagina". Sparks was transported to the hospital in a coma and suffered damages which continue to plague her.

However, she was one of the lucky few victims to survive an attack by Bundy.

Lynda Ann Healy, 21

A very accomplished and beautiful young woman, 21-year-old Lynda Healy announced ski conditions for all of the western Washington resorts on the radio. A senior at the University of Washington, she came from a good family, loved to sing, and was majoring in psychology. She shared a house with four other young women near the university. On 31 January, Healy and some friends went to a tavern and then home to bed. Her roommate in the next room never heard any sounds emanating from Healy's room that night.

The following morning when she didn't emerge from her bedroom after her alarm clock sounded at its usual 5:30 a.m. to go to work—and her job called looking for her—her roommate noticed that her bed was made in a peculiar way. Further inspection showed that the top sheet and a pillowcase were missing, a small bloodstain that was the same type as Lynda's was on the pillow and the bottom sheet, and a bloody nightgown was hanging in her closet. One of her outfits was missing. Also worrisome was that one of the doors was unlocked.

Initially, due to the absence of fingerprint, hair, or fiber evidence, police did not suspect foul play; however, later, they did come to realize that an intruder came in, removed Healy's nightgown and dressed her in another outfit, made the bed, wrapped her up, and took her out of the house.

Donna Gail Manson, 19

On 12 March, in Olympia, 19-year-old Evergreen State College student Donna Manson was kidnapped and murdered.

Susan Elaine Rancourt, 18

On 17 April, Susan Rancourt, 18, disappeared from the Central Washington State College campus in Ellensburg while walking across campus, alone, at night.

Later, two other female coeds would report meeting a good-looking man with his arm in a cast—one the night Rancourt disappeared and one three nights earlier—who asked for assistance with carrying books to his VW Beetle.

Roberta Kathleen "Kathy" Parks, 22

Kathy Parks, 22, was last seen on 6 May on the Oregon State University campus in Corvallis en route to meeting friends for coffee.

Brenda Carol Ball, 22

22-year-old Brenda Ball was last seen leaving the Flame Tavern in Burien, Oregon on 1 June.

Georgeann Hawkins, 18

In the early morning hours of 11 June, University of Washington student and a member of Kappa Alpha Theta Georgeann Hawkins, 18, left her boyfriend's dormitory en route to her sorority house through an alley. She was never seen again; however, witnesses later stated they had seen a man with a leg cast struggling to carry a briefcase in that area. Another female coed reported that he had asked her for help in carrying his briefcase to his VW Beetle.

Bundy later confessed to having lured Hawkins to his car, clubbed her with a tire iron he had hidden underneath his vehicle, and then took her elsewhere to rape and strangle her to death.

Janice Ann Ott, 23, and Denise Marie Naslund, 19

On 14 July, Janet Ott, 23, and Denise Naslund, 19, were abducted mere hours apart from Lake Sammamish State Park in Issaquah, Washington, in broad daylight. On that day, eight different witnesses reported seeing a handsome young man with his arm in a sling who called himself "Ted" and who asked several women for help unloading a sailboat from his VW Beetle. One witness said she walked with him for a ways but didn't see a sailboat and then declined to help him. Other witnesses stated that they saw the man approach Ott and she was observed walking away with him.

Naslund disappeared four hours later.

At this point, police in King County put up fliers with the suspected murderer's description all over the Seattle area. One of Bundy's psychology professors, former coworker Ann Rule, and Bundy's girlfriend Elizabeth Kloepfer reported him as a possible suspect. In fact, Kloepfer (who since changed her surname to Kendall and penned a book called *The Phantom Prince: My Life with Ted Bundy* in 1981) told the Seattle Police Department that her boyfriend "might be involved" in the recent Seattle murders. She called again later that autumn with more information and agreed to give them recent pictures of Bundy to be shown to witnesses; however, many of them could not positively identify him.

Ott's and Naslund's remains were found on 7 September off Interstate 90 near Issaquah, only one mile from the park where they were abducted. Near the women's remains was an extra femur and vertebrae which Bundy confessed before his execution belonged to Hawkins.

Between 1 March and 3 March 1975, the skulls and jawbones belonging to Healy, Rancourt, Parks, and Ball were found just east of Issaquah on Taylor Mountain. Bundy confessed in his death row interview that he kept the decapitated heads of these four victims in his apartment for some time and that he would revisit this dump site often to engage in sex with the corpses until decomposition became too great to continue. Bundy also admitted that he dumped Manson's body there as well—but burned her skull in his girlfriend's fireplace—however, no trace of her was ever recovered.

Other trophies discovered when Bundy's apartment was searched include photographs of his victims and a large bag of women's clothing.

Nancy Wilcox, 16

Bundy began the University of Utah Law School in the autumn of 1974. On 2 October 1974, 16-year-old Nancy Wilcox disappeared from Holladay, Utah. She was last seen in a VW Beetle.

Melissa Smith, 17

On 18 October, 17-year-old Melissa Smith—the daughter of Midvale, Utah's Police Chief Louis Smith—disappeared after leaving a pizza parlor. Nine days later she was found strangled, raped, and sodomized.

Laura Aime, 17

17-year-old Laura Aime disappeared from a Halloween party in Lehi, Utah. Her naked corpse was found on Thanksgiving Day by hikers near a river in the Wasatch Mountains. She had been beaten about the head and face with a crowbar and was raped and sodomized. The lack of blood at the crime scene indicated that she was likely killed elsewhere and dumped in this location. Police found no other physical evidence.

Carol DaRonch, 18 (survived)

On 8 November, 18-year-old Carol DaRonch was shopping at the Fashion Place Mall in Salt Lake City, Utah, and was approached by a man in the Sears parking lot who claimed to be a police officer named Officer Roseland. He told her that her car had been stolen and that he would take her to the police station to retrieve it. He took her to his VW Beetle and she became suspicious and asked him for identification. He quickly flashed a gold badge and she got in but refused his order to fasten her seat belt. After a short distance, Bundy pulled over and attempted to place handcuffs on DaRonch but only managed one wrist. He also attempted to hit her with a crowbar which she was able to catch before it hit her head. DaRonch fought back, kicking him in the groin, and as the car was speeding away she jumped out of it.

DaRonch flagged down another car and they took her to the police who confirmed there was no Officer Roseland. Police were able to obtain a description of the assailant and his car and a blood sample from DaRonch's coat. Type O; the same as Bundy's.

Debra Kent, 17

Mere hours after losing DaRonch Bundy abducted 17-year-old Debra "Debi" Kent from the parking lot of a school in Bountiful, Utah, as she was leaving a school play. She had told her parents she was going to pick up her brother at the bowling alley and she would be back to pick them up soon but never returned. She didn't even make it to her car which was still in the parking lot. Police found a small handcuff key in the parking lot and when they tried the key in the handcuffs DaRonch was wearing, it was a perfect fit.

A month later a man called the police and told them that he saw a tan VW Beetle speeding away from the high school parking lot the night Kent disappeared.

Shortly before he was to be executed, Bundy confessed that he dumped Kent's body near Fairview, Utah. After an intense search of the area, a human kneecap which was consistent with someone of Kent's age and size was found; however, DNA analysis was not conducted.

Caryn Campbell, 23

Bundy's first murder of 1975 occurred on 12 January. 23-year-old Michigan nurse Caryn Campbell disappeared between her hotel's lounge and her room while on a ski trip with her fiancé, Dr. Raymond Gadowski, and his two children, in Snowmass, Colorado. Frantic Gadowski called the police the next morning but a search proved futile.

Nearly a month later—and only a few short miles from where she went missing—a recreational worker discovered Campbell's nude body near the road. Animal damage to her body made it difficult to determine the exact cause of death; however, there was evidence of repeated, crushing blows to her head by a sharp instrument. Some of the blows were so violent that one of her teeth separated from the gums.

Julie Cunningham, 26

On 15 March, 26-year-old Vail ski instructor Julie Cunningham disappeared on her way to a nearby tavern. Bundy confessed in prison that he used his crutches ploy to approach Cunningham to ask for her help carrying ski boots to his car before he clubbed her with his crowbar, handcuffed her, and took her to a secluded location where strangled her.

Denise Oliverson, 25

25-year-old Denise Oliverson vanished in Grand Junction on 6 April while riding her bicycle to visit her parents.

Lynette Culver, 13

13-year-old Lynette Culver was abducted from her school playground at Alameda Junior High School in Pocatello, Idaho.

Susan Curtis, 15

Once Bundy returned to Utah, 15-year-old Susan Curtis vanished on 28 June while walking alone to the Brigham Young University dormitories during a youth conference she was attending. Bundy confessed to her murder minutes before his execution.

The bodies of Cunningham, Oliverson, Culver, and Curtis have never been found.

First Arrest, Trial, and Escapes

Bundy was first arrested on 16 August 1975 in Salt Lake City for failure to stop his vehicle for police. A search of his car unearthed a crowbar, handcuffs, ski mask, trash bags, an icepick, and other items the officer thought were burglary tools. The always calm and collected Bundy explained reasons why he had the items such as that he used the mask for skiing and had found the handcuffs in a dumpster; however, Detective Jerry Thompson connected Bundy and his Volkswagen to the DaRonch kidnapping and other missing girls and searched his apartment.

The search yielded a brochure of Colorado ski resorts with a checkmark by where Campbell had disappeared. Bundy was brought in for a lineup before DaRonch and other witnesses at the time DaRonch was kidnapped and they all identified him as Officer Roseland, as well as the man lurking about on the night Debbie Kent vanished.

After a week-long trial, Bundy was convicted on 1 March 1976 of kidnapping DaRonch and was sentenced to 15 years in Utah State Prison. Bundy was then extradited to Colorado to stand trial for murder.

He was able to escape custody twice before his eventual final arrest in Florida. The first escape occurred on 7 June 1977, when he was transported from the Garfield County Jail in Glenwood Springs, Colorado, to Pitkin County Courthouse in Aspen for his preliminary hearing. As he was serving as his own attorney, the judge excused him from being handcuffed and shackled. During a recess Bundy asked if he could research his case in the courthouse's law library. Hiding behind a bookcase he jumped from a second-story window, spraining his ankle when he landed. After shedding his suit, he simply walked through the town of Aspen as roadblocks were being erected before hiking southward on Aspen Mountain.

Near its summit he burglarized a cabin and stole clothing, food, and a rifle before heading toward Crested Butte; however, Bundy became lost and ended up wandering aimlessly for two days before breaking into a camping trailer on Maroon Lake where he took more food and a parka. Bundy then walked back toward Aspen and stole a car parked at the Aspen Golf Course. Two police officers noticed him weaving in traffic and pulled over the six-day fugitive. In the car were maps of the mountains around Aspen that the prosecutor was using to demonstrate where victim Caryn Campbell's body was found. As Bundy was his own attorney, he had the right of discovery to this evidence, thus demonstrating that he had planned his escape.

Bundy's second escape occurred on 30 December 1977, after having his motion for a change of venue to Denver accepted but with the venue being Colorado Springs instead; a city that had historically been hostile to murder suspects. He had managed to acquire the jail's floor plan and a hacksaw blade from other inmates, as well as $500 in cash smuggled in over a six-month period by visitors—particularly one Carole Ann Boone. In the evening while other inmates were showering, Bundy sawed a one-foot-square hole in his cell's ceiling—behind the steel bars—and was able to fit through it into the crawlspace above after losing 35 pounds. Prior to his actual escape, Bundy "practiced" and multiple reports of possible movement in the ceiling's crawlspace were, curiously, never investigated.

On the night of his escape, Bundy piled files and books under his covers in his bunk to look like his sleeping body, climbed into the crawlspace, broke through the jail's ceiling which, incidentally, was the chief jailer's apartment who just happened to be out for the evening with his wife. Bundy stole some street clothes and casually sauntered out the front door.

Bundy stole a car and drove east; however, the car broke down on Colorado's Interstate 70. A passing motorist gave him a ride into Vail where he caught a bus to Denver and then took a flight to Chicago, Illinois. From there he took an Amtrak train to Ann Arbor, Michigan.

His escape was discovered over 17 hours after the fact at noon on New Year's Eve.

Lisa Levy, 20, Margaret Bowman, 21, Karen Chandler (survived), Kathy Kleiner Deshields (survived)

On 15 January 1978—after Bundy had escaped from jail in Colorado, he traveled to Tallahassee, Florida, and attacked Chi Omega sorority sisters at Florida State University. At approximately 3:00 a.m. he entered the sorority house where he raped and strangled 20-year-old Lisa Levy to death; bludgeoned 21-year-old Margaret Bowman to death; and also bludgeoned Karen Chandler and Kathy Kleiner—both of whom survived.

The entire rampage took only 30 minutes.

Cheryl Thomas (survived)

That same morning, a mere eight blocks from the Chi Omega sorority house, Bundy attacked Cheryl Thomas in her bed and bludgeoned her with a wooden club, severely injuring her.

Kimberly Leach, 12

On 9 February, Bundy kidnapped 12-year-old Kimberly Leach from her junior high school in Lake City, Florida. Her raped, murdered, and dumped body was found in Suwannee River State Park underneath a small pig shed.

Bundy then stole another VW Beetle and left Tallahassee, traveling west across the Florida panhandle.

Florida Arrest

On 15 February 1978 shortly after 1:00 a.m., Bundy was stopped by Pensacola police officer David Lee who learned that the vehicle was stolen. After a brief scuffle, Lee had subdued and restrained Bundy and then took him to jail. During the transport, Bundy allegedly told Lee that he wished the officer would have killed him. Once his identity was confirmed, Bundy was transported to Tallahassee and charged with the Tallahassee and Lake City murders.

Florida Trials and Convictions

Among the most damning evidence during Bundy's June 1979 Chi Omega murder trial were bite marks found on Lisa Levy's left buttock which matched a plaster cast taken from Bundy's mouth. Additionally, Chi Omega sister Nita Neary was returning home late that night and saw Bundy as he left. She was able to identify him in court.

Bundy was convicted on all counts and sentenced to death.

In 1980, Bundy stood trial for the Kimberly Leach murder. Again, he was convicted, this time based upon fiber evidence and an eyewitness who saw him leading Leach away from the school. Bundy was, again, sentenced to death.

After his sentences he sought a stay of execution or commutation of his death sentences to life imprisonment by having one of his legal advocates contact his victims' families to ask them to ask for mercy in order to find out where their loved ones' remains were. This ploy for more time failed.

Execution

Bundy ultimately met his demise in Raiford Prison's electric chair on 24 January 1989.

Shortly before his widely-publicized execution, Bundy confessed to 36 murders in seven states; however, many believe that the total number is much higher. Also before his execution, Bundy contacted Dr. James Dobson, psychologist and founder of the Christian evangelical organization Focus on the Family, and agreed to a television interview the day before his execution. In it, Bundy described the influence of pornography on his behavior. While not expressly blaming pornography for his behavior, Bundy did say that pornographic materials shaped and molded his behavior and he would gradually need more violent, graphic, and explicit material to achieve the same "high"; not unlike a drug addict. He claimed that while murdering he was "possessed by 'something ... awful and alien'" and the brutal urge was indescribable. He also claimed that alcohol helped remove the initial boundary for him to commit his first murder. Bundy also admitted that although he believed he deserved the death penalty, he didn't want to die.

Even today, Bundy remains a suspect in a number of open homicide cases and is likely responsible for other victims who will never be identified. In 1987 he confided to Keppel that there were some murders that he would "never talk about" because they were committed too close to home, involved victims who were very young, or were too close to family. Said victims include the aforementioned Ann Marie Burr who Bundy repeatedly denied having murdered; however, Keppel noticed that Burr fits all three of Bundy's "no discussion" categories. In 2011, forensic testing of material from the Burr crime scene did not have enough intact DNA sequences to compare to Bundy's.

Additional potential victims include flight attendants Lisa E. Wick and Lonnie Trumbull, both 20, who were bludgeoned with a piece of wood while asleep in their Seattle home on 23 June 1966 that was very near the Safeway store where Bundy worked at the time, and where the victims regularly shopped. Trumbull did not make it and Wick suffered permanent memory loss.

On 30 May 1969 college friends Susan Davis and Elizabeth Perry, both 19, who were on vacation in Atlantic City, New Jersey—just 60 miles south of Philadelphia—were found stabbed to death in the woods three days later.

On 19 July 1971, 24-year-old elementary school teacher and motel maid Rita Curran was murdered in her basement apartment in Burlington, Vermont. She had been bludgeoned, raped, and strangled. The motel where she worked part-time was adjacent to the Elizabeth Lund Home where Bundy was born and certain similarities to his other crime scenes made Bundy a suspect.

21-year-old Joyce LePage was last seen alive on 22 July 1971 on the Washington State University campus. Nine months later her skeleton was found wrapped in military blankets, carpeting, and rope, at the bottom of a Pullman, Washington, ravine.

On 29 June 1973, 17-year-old Rita Lorraine Jolly disappeared from West Linn, Oregon while 24-year-old Vicki Lynn Hollar disappeared from Eugene, Oregon, on 20 August of that same year. Bundy had confessed to two Oregon homicides but did not identify the victims.

Brenda Joy Baker, 14, was last seen hitchhiking near Puyallup, Washington on 27 May 1974 and her body would be discovered a month later in Millersylvania State Park.

19-year-old Wisconsin native Sandra Jean Weaver who had been living in Tooele, Utah, was last seen on 1 July 1974 in Salt Lake City. Her nude body was found the following day in Grand Junction, Colorado.

20-year-old Carol Valenzuela was last seen hitchhiking near Vancouver, Washington, on 2 August 1974 and her remains were found two months later in a shallow grave south of Olympia; along with the remains of another female who was later identified as 17-year-old Martha Morrison who was last seen in Eugene, Oregon, on 1 September 1974. During this time, Bundy drove from Seattle to Salt Lake City and could have conceivably passed through both towns; however, there is no definitive evidence.

Bundy is also a suspect in Melanie Suzanne Cooley's disappearance on 15 April 1975 after leaving Nederland High School in Nederland, Colorado. Her beaten and strangled corpse was discovered on 2 May by road maintenance workers nearby in Coal Creek Canyon. Whereas gas receipts place Bundy in Golden that day—not far from Nederland—the Jefferson County Sheriff's Office has classified her murder as a cold case.

On 1 July 1975, Shelly Kay Robertson, 24, failed to show up for work in Golden, Colorado, and her nude, decomposed corpse was found in August inside of a mine on Berthoud Pass near Winter Park. While gas station receipts place Bundy in the area, there is no direct evidence as to his complicity.

23-year-old Nancy Perry Baird disappeared from the Farmington, Utah, service station where she worked on 4 July 1975. She officially remains a missing person and Bundy has repeatedly denied involvement.

Finally, 17-year-old Debbie Smith was last seen in February 1976 in Salt Lake City before the DaRonch trial. Her body was found near the airport on 1 April 1976.

Aftermath

During the Kimberly Leach trial, Bundy married Carole Ann Boone. He took advantage of an existing Florida statute in which a marriage declaration in court in front of a judge constituted a legal marriage. Thus, Bundy called Boone as a character witness and married her while she was on the witness stand. After numerous conjugal visits, Boone gave birth to a daughter in October 1982. She returned to Washington in 1986 with her daughter after divorcing him and never returned.

Ann Rule described Bundy as "... a sadistic sociopath who took pleasure from another human's pain and the control he had over his victims, to the point of death, and even after." He once referred to himself as "the most cold-hearted son of a bitch you'll ever meet" and one of his defense attorneys, Polly Nelson, said that Bundy "was the very definition of heartless evil." At one point, Bundy said, "We serial killers are your sons, we are your husbands, we are everywhere. And there will be more of your children dead tomorrow."

Bundy contacted Robert Keppel—the detective who helped put him in prison—while on death row to assist him with the "Green River Killer" investigation at the time. With Bundy's assistance, Keppel was able to understand the inner workings of the mind of a serial killer and was, subsequently, able to identify and apprehend Gary Ridgway in November 2001.

Ted Bundy has been the subject of three television movies and one feature film. The two-part film entitled *The Deliberate Stranger* aired on NBC in 1986, starring Mark Harmon as Bundy. *Ted Bundy* (2002) starred Michael Reilly Burke as Bundy and was directed by Matthew Bright. In 2003 the USA Network aired Ann Rule's *The Stranger Beside Me* that starred Billy Campbell as Bundy and Barbara Hershey as Rule. Finally, the A&E network produced an adaptation of detective Robert Keppel's book *The Riverman* in 2004, starring Cary Elwes as Bundy and Bruce Greenwood as Keppel.